T0354313

124 DAYS OF

Hope and Healing

TEREASA CHATHAM

BALBOA.PRESS

A DIVISION OF HAY HOUSE

Balboa Press books may be ordered through booksellers or by contacting:

Balboa Press
A Division of Hay House
1663 Liberty Drive
Bloomington, IN 47403
www.balboapress.com.au
1 (877) 407-4847

Print information available on the last page.

ISBN: 978-1-5043-2127-3 (sc)
ISBN: 978-1-5043-2126-6 (e)

Balboa Press rev. date: 04/07/2020

Contents

Acknowledgements

Without the following people, I would not have found the balance to think both logically and emotionally on this journey.

♡ A huge heartfelt thank you goes to Uncle Petie and Aunty Lee Lee. Your unconditional love and support for me both spiritually and emotionally has me truly grateful to Dad for bringing you into my life twenty-five years ago, before he passed. You were a channel for his guidance that I hadn't yet opened to listening to. I enjoyed our Sunday night "bus stop" catch up to grab a homemade dinner for the kids and myself, a cuddle, and always a good laugh. You listened to my way out there comments and always gave valued opinions. You never made me feel like I was crazy or misunderstood. I love you both. You are earth angels sent to me from the heavens above!

♡ To Leon,

I will never again underestimate the universal push/pull. There are no coincidences.

I met you late last year, after offering to help your son sew. My guides told me at the time, "You are getting more than you could ever imagine with this family. Brace yourself!" When my husband went down, and I called you to cancel my sewing lesson with your son and the reason, you never stepped back but checked in on my hubby, the kids, and me daily.

Your emotional support and your advice, based on your life experiences, helped me stay grounded. You always played the devil's advocate and helped me see the logic when I ran on too much emotion. You never verbalised how crazy you thought my comments may have been, but I do feel that your eyes rolled a lot. Even I was surprised at some of the things that came out of my mouth.

Thank you for always listening and just being you!

♡ To our amazing, self-appointed project manager, Andrew,

Thank you for stepping up from the very first day and taking charge of the logistics of this journey. We have never asked for help throughout our thirty years, and when you took control in the background without hesitation, it was very much appreciated. You stated from the very get-go, "You only did what Chatham would have done in this situation." I have often said Conrad hand-selected his team, and I am very grateful to you being one of his best choices. You organised a huge cookout, a boot camp fundraiser, and a Go Fund Me campaign. You finished off projects at home without hesitation, along with turning up weekly to support Conrad, the kids, and I at the hospital. You are "good people."

Thank you.

♡ To our three amazing young adults,

I always tried to protect you by hiding the "real world" from you. And in doing that, I also hid my true self. I felt I wasn't normal and didn't want to burden you with a weird, crazy mum. Or should I say crazier than you already thought.

I thank you all for sitting and listening to me on the very first day of this journey and trusting me enough to step outside society expectations and medical logic to explore alternative options for your dad. You opened your hearts to trust me, and in doing so, it opened up my trust in myself. I am so grateful for this learning and how we have become closer as a family. In times like this you realise who is there for the tough times and who is on your team. Dad and I are very proud of the three beautiful adults we have raised. You all amaze me with your strength, compassion, support, and so much more.

I love you all to the moon and back!

♡ To my soul mate,

Where do I start?

Thank you for letting go but also for fighting. Thank you for showing vulnerability and emotion but also strength and logic.

Your soul chose your team members for this journey before you actually knew it. I thank you for choosing me to be the captain of your team.

I've often said, "The bigger the hurt, the bigger the heal," and, "The bigger the lesson, the bigger the learning." Well the hurt we experienced when you went down fades in comparison to the healing you did on this journey. And the lessons I have taken from this experience have changed my life for the better.

I found strength in your weakness, and I found laughter amongst our tears. As sad and hard as this journey has been, I found happiness, peace, and understanding. But most of all, I found myself!

I wholeheartedly thank you for your willingness to open up and let your team find the right tools for you to fight. Whether it be medical or metaphysical, you had a "tool box" as big as a Bunnings store (as Aunty Lee Lee used to say), and you showed our kids what it takes to rise above. Anything is possible!

♡ Last but not least,

Thank you to my angels, my guides (in particular, Dad and Nanna Chatham), my higher self, and the universe. I am finally listening and now writing.

Introduction

Empathy—the ability to understand and share the feelings of another.

Narcissist—self-important, inability to show compassion and empathy.

Empaths—highly sensitive individuals who have a keen ability to sense what people around them are thinking and feeling. They have the ability to physically feel and experience what another person is going through.

Intuition—the ability to acquire knowledge without proof, evidence, or conscious reasoning, or without understanding how the knowledge was acquired.

Intuitive empath—a person with an unusual capacity for sensing and understanding the feelings of others. They have the ability to know what others feel without needing to be told.

- 5 per cent of people are narcissists, lack compassion and empathy, and don't show emotion.
- 80 per cent to 90 per cent of people have compassion and empathy and feel their own emotions.
- 10 per cent to 15 per cent of people are empaths. They feel their own and others' emotions.

The above is based on my research and understanding.

Hi.

My name is Tereasa Chatham.

I am an intuitive empath. I feel the feel!

I have a gift!

My role is currently that of a forty-seven-year-old mum of three young amazing adults and a wife to Conrad. I have been with my husband for thirty-one years and married twenty-five years as of August 2019.

I have spent almost thirty years learning about essential oils and crystals and their healing properties. More recently, I have been learning about metaphysics and quantum. I had not fully shared this passion with my family or others for fear of criticism.

On January 17, 2019, my husband had a cardiac arrest, and our whole world changed. This story is my journey and my perception of events over the 124 days that my husband was in hospital.

I have always had a positive attitude no matter what gets thrown at me. And one of my biggest assets is my sense of humour—as bad as some feel it may be. I am grateful of the lessons that I have taken away from this journey. I've often used the quote, "Every cloud has a silver lining." I feel you just need to find the positive in any situation, no matter how negative the event at the time.

I feel every single thing is a foundation for something, whether it be a word to make a sentence, chapters to make a book, people we meet, or situations we are in. There are no coincidences in life. Everything is a foundation for something. We just may not realise it at the time.

This book is raw and may not sit well with everyone. I am very "out there" from the normal and often boring way of thinking. And I am unapologetically me. This is what gets me through life. So in advance, I will not apologise for who I am.

I swear, and I laugh—often at the most inappropriate times. I will do my best to not step over offensive lines, but my line may not necessarily be sitting at the same place as yours. And that's okay. You don't have to keep reading.

My reason for writing this book? To give people hope.

Never give up without being fully comfortable with your decision, and always trust your inner guidance.

Foundations

Finally, after twenty-five years, I decided I was going to do a course I have wanted to do since my late teens: tantra!

It popped up at me as a point of interest for years, but when I approached my husband about doing the course when I was twenty, his determined reply had been, "No, you just don't want to have sex with me." I didn't know what tantra was at that time, but maybe he did, so I let it go.

It popped up again through the years, and I started to do a little more research about the topic. Most avenues lead to sex, but they did not resonate with me. There had to be more.

In January 2017, it hit me again in a Facebook post. This time, the person running the education course on tantra captured my interest. I felt she was the right person to guide me on my path. I did further research on the Sanctuary of Ananda and found her principles and gentleness resonated with me. After months of conversation with Catherine Wood, the founder, I made the decision to go to Bali and find out more about this subject.

When I again approached Conrad on this, he was adamant that I was not going. He expressed all his concerns about why I shouldn't attend: It was a foreign country, it was tantra, I was going to put our family at risk if I left the country. The list went

1

on and on. But not once did he ask *why* I wanted to do it. For thirty years, I had been the dutiful wife and mother and always put my family first. The time had come to finally step into my own. I was tired of doing as I was told and complying to the rules at work, at home, and with family. Don't get me wrong. I loved my family and what we had accomplished. And we never argued. I always bit my tongue and just went with the flow.

As the time came closer to locking in my tickets, Conrad got angrier. I didn't understand what his reservations were as he still didn't know what I wanted to do. He just thought I was being defiant and, God forbid, leaving the country and, therefore, taking a risk!

The more he disagreed, the more determined I was to finally do something for myself. I arranged my birth certificate and passport, and again tried to get his approval. In March, and after several approaches on the subject, I had enough. So the five-day course that I had advised I was attending became a day longer every time he said I couldn't go.

I said, "I'm going for five days."

"No, you are not."

"It's now six days."

"No, you are not."

"Seven."

"No."

"Eight."

The very next day, flights were booked for ten days in Bali.

I was determined to make this happen, so I worked extra hours to pay for flights, accommodation, and spending money. I didn't want to put extra financial pressure on the family or fuel the fire that was already burning in the background. I enlisted a girlfriend to try and plead my case to Conrad. (Thanks, Tania.)

After several weeks, he finally accepted the decision and became more agreeable. So much so that for my birthday the week before I flew out, he actually gave me a million dollars in Bali money. He boasted at the fact he gave me a million dollars. It equated to $100 AUD, but it certainly made me feel that he had finally accepted my decision.

I stepped off the plane on June 10, 2017, and burst into tears. This was an amazingly overwhelming experience for me in several ways. I had landed in a foreign country, I knew nobody, and I had defied my husband. This was *huge!*

Over the next five days, Catherine shared her understanding of tantra based on Tao Buddhism and showed us meditations, massages, and practices to raise our vibrational frequencies to a higher conscious awareness. I took away the following: Tantra is a way of life and a discipline. It is about universal balance, and everyone's journey is different. I was excited to grow in this space. The more time has gone by, the more I feel that tantra is just that—a way of life. And everyone's journey is different. So when I read a book or see an article, I know what I am reading is someone's perception and understanding of tantra, and no individual's way is right or wrong. It is that individual's path.

Every day I awoke in Bali I couldn't wipe the smile off my face. I was like a sponge, absorbing every tiny detail: the surroundings, the culture, the course, the people. This was life-changing. When I returned home, I couldn't explain what I had learned in a way that was understandable to my eagerly awaiting family.

Tantra helped me see the balances—even and uneven—in my life. It helped me understand my behaviours and let me see what destructive or unhealthy patterns I had. I approached my hubby and told him that one of my unhealthy behaviours was poker machines. I felt that I went to the poker machines on a weekend to find my emotional "out." I had been married to my husband for almost twenty-five years (and we had been together for thirty), and I felt he was emotionally unavailable to me. I knew very little about his childhood, and he never showed emotion. I had never seen him cry, and he rarely expressed softness. He showed other emotions, like frustration or anger, if the time was right, but to sit and discuss personal or sensitive issues? Forget it! I was a very touchy-feely person and wanted to share this with Conrad. I didn't push for him to open up, but I wanted him to at least listen when I had concerns, such as when I found lumps in my breast.

Don't get me wrong; I loved my husband, and he was a good, decent person. He committed, wholeheartedly, to the community and work. He was very good at what he did, and his motto at work was, "Rarely ever wrong!" This was also very much his life's motto. As Conrad was so structured and strong in his values, he could be seen as quite emotionally hard. We had come up with the comment of 10 per cent softer, that's all we asked, and his workplace was the same, both work and home often laughed when he made reference to this. He always seemed to have control of any situation. This was especially great for his role as a finance and operations manager and president of the local cricket club. In business and society, there are advantages to being so strong and direct, but when it comes to love and life, the same doesn't always work unless someone plays a lesser role. In the relationship, and over time, this was not healthy for me and our relationship.

I have always been a little crafty and hands-on, but after my trip to Bali, I felt a strong need to make quilts for each of the kids. It resonated with me to make these in what I call a "chakra theme." The body has seven energy fields known as chakras. Each has a different colour and a different role within our bodies. Each chakra also has an essential oil and a crystal that resonates with it and enhances its abilities.

For ten months I worked on creating a quilt that represented me and what I wanted for each of my children. The energy that I put into this first quilt was overwhelming at times. It was such a strong and loving energy that it felt good just to touch it. When the quilt was almost finished, I felt I needed to infuse it with both crystals and essential oils. I embroidered the words of each crystal and each oil and placed the related oil and crystal on it on our pool table for a couple of days.

I was very proud as it was my first quilt. It represented me and all that I was passionate about: sewing, crystals, oil, and love. On completion of the quilt on Mother's Day 2018, I finally showed Conrad my masterpiece. I handed it to him, and he dropped it on the floor. He immediately asked, "What have you done to it? I have the hairs on my back standing up!"

I laughed. "It's a *healing* quilt."

He walked off, laughing and shaking his head. It became a joke. Anytime he came near my office and that quilt, I threw it at him and received the same reaction each time.

October 2017

After my return from Bali, my mind was racing. I was learning so much about myself and what I call "the universal game." Everything had to be in balance: black/white, day/night, emotion/logic, yin/yang. The list went on and on. But there was no one that I could sit and talk to about what was important to me. I tried to explain what I was feeling to my family, but on several occasions, they told me I was crazy and would get myself locked up if I kept talking and thinking the way I was. But in my mind, it was real and all made sense. I tried for weeks to open up and talk about what I learnt in Bali and what thoughts I had been having, but it always fell on deaf ears. I was often criticised or laughed at.

My husband spent so much time at the cricket club as the president, a coach, and a player. He devoted so many hours to obtaining government grants and sponsorships that it consumed his whole life. I couldn't sit and have a conversation with him that wasn't about cricket. I loved his commitment and enjoyed the sport; I spent weekends watching and helping in the canteen. But I was starting to resent the time it took from the family and me. The more time he spent at the cricket, unconsciously knowing at the time, the more time I spent at the pokies when I wasn't at work. I didn't enjoy my time there. I certainly didn't enjoy the money I wasted in them, and I wasn't addicted. I just didn't want to go home! My young-adult children all worked and had social lives. So I would walk into to an empty house that often had washing on the lounge and dishes in the sink. No matter how much I wanted to come home, it became harder. And I was becoming more miserable and lonely. I was not addicted to poker machines. I never woke up trying to find a way to get there at the end of the day. I genuinely drove home with good intentions but got to the end of my street and didn't want to turn left. It was a daily battle that I hated. And the more time that went by, the more money I wasted and the angrier I got at the whole situation. But again, I had no one to talk to. I had tried in July to explain to my husband why I went to the pokies. Most weekends I suggested we go out to listen to music or to a movie, but after a long week and the commitments he had, it would be a no, and he would be asleep on the lounge by 7:30, while I sat alone, watching the TV. Or I would go to the club by myself to play pokies. It was a vicious cycle.

On October 8, 2017, my husband finally realised something wasn't right based on my behaviours, and he started to follow his instincts. Something was amiss, but he couldn't figure it out. He finally got to looking at our bank account and thought, *WTF?* For thirty years, I had asked him to help with finances and bills, but his reply was always, "I have enough hassle at work. I don't need it at home." He had full access to everything and was a fantastic finance manager at work but never managed ours. To say the sh*t hit the fan that day would be an understatement. When I got his email at work asking, "Who's account is this?" the reply was "Mine." The first thought I had was, *I am dead.* But it was the biggest relief, and I was ready to face the music. Bring it on!

I gladly handed over all my key cards and walked into the banks where I held accounts and closed them immediately. I took the kids with me and advised the banking staff I had a gambling problem and needed to close all access to funds. I stood up and owned my actions 100 per cent. I was fully accountable for the consequences of my behaviours, but to try and explain to my family what and why I had done what I did was my biggest task. I was verbally abused, humiliated, and had to account for my whereabouts daily. And I had to sit in front of my children and answer any questions that were put to me. This was just the tip of the iceberg. Nightly, my husband would lie awake processing what I had done. He would wake me to question me for hours on hours to get the same answers. I was exhausted. Finally, we decided on a marriage counsellor to discuss our situation. We agreed on the same counsellor who helped us years earlier, when our daughter suffered anorexia nervosa.

Our weekly meeting bought mixed emotions for me. I was excited at the possibility of moving forward. But I also came to dread the trip home as my husband would yell at me and get quite angry at the discussions we had at each meeting. I was grateful at being able to express myself, no matter how much backlash I received. Conrad, on the other hand, felt I was deliberately causing more issues by discussing topics that were not related to what I had done that instigated the counselling session.

I have always had the mentality to "Never regret what you do, but you need to learn from your mistakes." As much as this hurt my family, it was one of the biggest learning experiences and actually brought our family closer together in the long run. The broken trust was my saddest and only regret. The money, to me, was materialistic, and it was worth it to have my family brought together.

No matter how much I tried to explain myself, it fell on deaf ears. My husband is very much black and white; there are no grey areas in his mind. I often commented that if we both walked into a bar and someone was drunk at the counter, he would automatically categorise that person as a drunk, and I would see the look of disgust on his face whenever we were in that situation. I, on the other hand, would wonder if the person just lost his or her partner, been diagnosed with an illness, or if this was the first time to the bar and that person's way of dealing with whatever life threw at him or her. I make a conscious effort never to judge a person. I am not in the other person's shoes, so I do not know why someone did what he or she did.

Over the years I have learned that we tend to run away from our problems when we can't deal with them. Some people turn to drugs, alcohol, or sex. I turned to gambling. I am very mindful and know I am not addicted, and I made the conscious decision not to replace one bad habit with another. Therefore I can proudly say that I have not had a drink since September 26, 2017, and I have not been to a poker machine since October 6, 2017.

June 2018

It started with a shortness of breath and a heavy chest. Then visions of a heart and then of my mother and mother-in-law, and both were alone. I sat on this for a few days, wondering, *Am I going crazy? I can't explain this to anybody. Who would believe me?* Over the next few days, the feelings and visions got stronger and more frequent. Then I started tasting blood with the shortness of breath. I had to tell someone, but who was not going to laugh at me? Finally, I bit the bullet and said to Conrad, "Babe, I know this is going to sound crazy, but …" As I explained my visions and sensations, dates came through of late September early October, but I couldn't tell if it was my mum's husband or my father-in-law; they were overlapping in my mind. Conrad didn't engage in the conversation; he just listened. A seed had been planted, and that was all I could do. If nothing came of this, great. But if it did, we may be a little less surprised.

September 2018

In late September, Conrad started to experience chest pains, and after I pushed him for several days, he finally went to the doctor. Our doctor put him straight into an ambulance to have it investigated. After many tests and a recall a week later for a stress test, he was given the all clear and sent home.

A day later, I got a distressed call from my mother. Her husband had been admitted to hospital with coronary heart disease and needed a quadruple bypass. I drove twelve hours south to be with my mum. (She has rheumatoid arthritis, and her husband is her carer.) Mum explained that he had been short of breath and was getting puffed very easily. He went to the doctor and was admitted immediately. He was operated on that week and recovered very well for a seventy-year-old. I drove home after a week, and the uneasy feeling returned—along with tasting blood and shortness of breath. I called my mother-in-law to check on them to be told Conrad's dad had been admitted to hospital that day with some sort of infection. Conrad and I drove west to make sure his mum was okay and to take her into town to be with his dad.

I had visions of his dad's parents (who have passed over) just holding hands and waiting. I felt this was a sign of how serious things could be. I still tasted blood and had shortness of breath. We arrived at the hospital, and his dad seemed fairly comfortable in a room of two. He said doctors weren't sure what was wrong, but he should be okay and discharged at any time. I watched him as he talked and saw increased colour in his cheeks as he got more tired. Conrad and his mum thought it best to let him rest and suggested we go for a coffee. Something didn't sit right with me. I felt his forehead as he started to make himself comfortable for a sleep. I went to the nurses' station and requested that they take his vitals and check his temperature. The nurse advised they were due to do this in about fifteen minutes and would be there shortly. I requested again and mentioned I felt he was running a temperature. After several requests, the nurse agreed. I caught up to Conrad and his mum to go for a coffee.

On our return an hour later, we found that Conrad's dad had been moved to another floor, and this time closer to the nurses' station, and was now on intravenous drugs for a severe infection. When I told Conrad that his grandparents were around and that I felt he didn't realise how close he was to losing his dad, he just looked at me. I knew he heard me, but it took a bit to sink in.

It turned out his dad had a serious lung infection that was linked to potting mix. His doctor didn't expect to see him again after he called the ambulance.

Both dads recovered well, thankfully.

An acquaintance I met twelve to eighteen months before started to pop into my mind. Then out of the blue, one night she called me. As I picked up the phone, I thought, *That's funny. I was thinking of calling Lorna to say hi and see how she was doing.*

It turned out that Lorna had recently visited a doctor—Dr Alt, short for Alternate—on the Gold Coast for her food intolerances, and while in her appointment, she felt I was there the whole time, knocking on her head, saying, "Hello, I'm here, and I need to meet this person." When she told me this, we both laughed. She went on to explain that she had an appointment that week with the same doctor, but she had no way of getting there as she was not confident in driving so far. Without hesitation, I offered to take her. This was not usually me as work always came first unless a day off was planned well in advance. The offer was accepted, and I wasn't going to let her down.

I drove to the Gold Coast, and when we got there, Lorna requested I go into the appointment with the doctor's approval. This doctor resonated with me immediately, and I wanted to know more about what she did. Her title noted she was, "Holistic and Integrative Medical Practitioner." She mentioned an upcoming workshop for empaths. Lorna and I locked into the course straight away and decided to make a weekend of it. At this workshop, I felt I was on the right path to finally understanding who I was. This same workshop had a gentleman who spoke intensely about the brain and quantum science. Most of what he said went way over my head, but he stated, "You can remap the neuropathways of the brain for almost any ailment." (At a later date, I realised why this statement stayed in my mind.) At the end of the day's session, he walked the group out to the car park and said, "Welcome to your new life."

The weekend away really opened my mind to a lot of unexplainable things. I started to feel that there was a lot more outside medical logic when it came to people and illness. I am very fortunate to not have had a pharmaceutical script for over twenty years; I have always turned to my essential oils and crystals if unwell. Lorna and I popped into a crystal shop down that way, and I picked up a few crystals for my collection. On the way out the door, there was a wheelbarrow full of a crystal that I had never heard of, and it resonated with me. So I bought a nice piece in the shape of a large, smooth sausage and about as long as my hand. It was called scolecite, and it looked and felt very calming and smooth to me. I thought it would be a lovely crystal to use for my massage therapy. Another one for the collection.

After that weekend, I had a need to investigate further higher awareness on all levels. The more I opened my way of thinking, the more it fascinated me and felt right. I started to research and put my own understanding on the universe, life lessons, and balances. I strongly felt that if we were to get an internal illness that is not DNA but something progressive, an emotional block could be the underlying cause and, in turn, eventually show up in the form of a symptom. Stay with me here; I'm not totally crazy.

Chinese medicine states that our bodies have natural clocks, and each of our body organs has a time that it repairs itself. There is also a sense linked to the organ, an emotion, and a symptom. I started to research this. It really started to excite me, so I looked further.

I started to map this in what I called "emotional decoding." And when I broke this down further, I started to see a much bigger picture, and it really took on a whole new perspective for me that expanded my already out there thought process.

For example,

Organ	Emotion	Symptom	Sense	Time
Liver/ Gallbladder	Anger, lack of courage, inability to make decisions, shock	Chest distension, bitter taste, jaundice, menstrual problems, breast tenderness	Eyes	11 p.m. to 1 a.m. (GB) 1 a.m. to 3 a.m. (LV)

Using myself and the above example, I am often awake between 1 a.m. and 3 a.m. I have an inability to make decisions, menstrual and breast problems, and my eyes? We won't go there! My liver is in need of some assistance.

October 2018

Another vision started to pop into my mind. This time a lightning bolt coming at me! Okay, now I'm listening. I have a sickening feeling in my belly and hear a voice say, "Brace yourself!" Hmm, now you have my undivided attention.

One beautiful Sunday I popped into Spotlight, my favourite hangout. I sat at the pattern table and saw a young man and his dad opposite. I smiled and thought, *That's lovely.* I felt the stress in the young man as he tried to explain to his dad what his intentions were in the pattern he was looking at. His dad was not as confident in his son's abilities, but he was very patient and respectful with his response. I smiled and whispered to the young man, "If anyone told me I couldn't do something, it only made me more determined," at which he laughed. Another customer came along and tried to direct him to having to use a pattern if he wanted it right. I, on the other hand, was never taught to sew and respectfully tried to give him two points of view because I often made my clothes ad hoc as a teenager. I can't say it was right, but it worked for me!

The whole time I sat there, my inner self kept saying, *You need to offer to help this person sew.* If anyone external had heard the internal battle in my head of my, *No, I do not have time to do this*" reply to *Yes you do. Make the time. You need to help this family,* they would have locked me up. I finally relented and handed the dad my business card, saying, "If he gets stuck, call me, and I will redirect him. If he has a talent and a passion, nurture it, and keep his mind off other things." The little voice in my head started again. *Not enough. You need to offer to help this person.* Again I replied, No, I don't have time, and I walked off to the counter to pay for my patterns. I had done my bit. Hadn't I? I offered to help. *Nope, not enough* was the reply in my head. I then saw the dad in the line beside me, and again the voices were at me. *You need to offer to help teach him to sew."* Fine then. I introduced myself to the dad and said, "This is going to sound odd, but if you would like me to help your son sew, I am happy to give him an hour a week, if time permits, to help him with his passion, at no cost" His dad replied, "I will let you know. I have your card. You do realise he has special needs, don't you?" I replied, "Yes, I do know that. I may be able to help you." I looked up with a silent, *Fine. Are you happy now? I offered!* And the reply came, *Yes. Thank you.*

Within a week, I received a call from the dad to help his son learn to sew. I started that next week to guide him with his costume. On the way to his house, the voices started chatting again. *Brace yourself. You are getting so much more here with this family.* "Whatever," was my reply, said with love, of course.

Over the next eight to twelve weeks, the images of that lightning bolt got stronger and appeared more often. I started to get an uneasy feeling, and in my mind, I was running to figure it out. Initially, my thoughts were of me not being true to myself, my hosting a workshop on eating disorders and focusing on setting up my business of being an alternate life Coach. I started to push for all the above, thinking, *I'm on the right track.* But no matter how much I pushed forward, these uneasy feelings and visions would not go away. I started to focus on my workshop, and dates started to pop up as pivotal. In my mind, the dates kept pulling me to mid-January, but I kept overruling this and pushing them out further and further. When I was booking the venue for my first workshop, the seventeenth of January kept coming at me. But in my head, this was too close for me to organise a workshop, and I reluctantly settled on January 21, 2019, though I still felt this was too close. I left the venue thinking, *I have six weeks to get myself sorted.* This worried me as the lightning bolt stayed firmly in my head as a vision.

December 2018

I could see my husband was putting a lot of pressure on himself with work and cricket, and I started to worry about him burning out. Over the previous twelve months, he had issues in one form or another at home, work, and cricket. He told me that he could not let go of a situation until he had put all his, "puzzle pieces together," and if he felt there was a piece missing, he would not let it go. He could not have closure. A situation arose from the previous administration that he struggled with ethically, and he would not let it go. I saw the same behaviour patterns in him that were very present in October 2017, when I went to the poker machines. At that time, he spent hours on hours going through every bank account of ours from the previous twelve months and spreadsheeted every single dollar I had spent. This included me taking $20 out at Coles. In his mind, and his words, I had spent upwards of fifty, seventy, a hundred thousand dollars. This figure rose daily in his comments to and accusations at me. He could not close off what I had done. Nor could he forgive me until he felt he had everything right in his mind. There was no way I could have spent the funds he noted as we didn't have them. But no matter how I tried to defend myself, he did not have his puzzle pieces, and I had no ability to prove otherwise.

One night sitting on the lounge, he turned to me and asked, "Why do all these things happen to me?" In his request, he was trying to figure out why he had issues at work, in the community, and at home.

I started off by saying, "If it hits a chord in what I say, this is when you need to really go deep and process what in it needs to be acknowledged before you dismiss me." I felt and explained that my take was, "The universe gives us lessons in everything we do. And if we do not learn the lesson in one situation, it presents itself in one form or another with the same underlying tone until we finally learn." I felt he had high expectations of people, and you cannot change or control people to do things your way, no matter how right he felt it was. It was a control issue that he needed to let go of. Just because it did not get done the way he would have done it, doesn't mean it was wrong. I mentioned that until he learned to let go of the control, those lessons would continue to come at him, and each lesson would get bigger. The examples I gave went way back to when we were teenagers, and he was a manager in retail. And to the more recent, as in our daughter with anorexia, my gambling, work, football, and cricket. All of these came back to the same emotional lesson and control for him. At first, he sat quietly, and credit to him, he listened to me. I think he actually processed my thoughts on this. Usually this would have brought a reaction from him.

In mid-December, after chatting with the kids about an idea I had, I suggested Conrad take advantage of his accrued long service leave and take some time to find himself, to take six, eight, ten, or however many weeks he needed to recharge and spend some quality time fishing and relaxing. I suggested he take the next few weeks just planning a trip to wherever he felt he wanted to go. I suggested I fly to meet him during this time, but he got angry and felt I was pushing him away. All I was trying to do was help him be closer to himself. I tried to explain that his whole life he put others first and didn't actually know who he was. He moved out of his parents' home at nineteen and became a retail manager, husband, father, sports vice president and president, and a business manager, to name a few. But in all this time, he never spent time with himself. He didn't know who he was when I asked the question, "Who is Conrad Chatham?" He rattled off his roles in life. When he asked me who I was, I smiled and replied, "I know I have many roles, but at my core, I am an empath, and I am unconditional. I may be more, and I am still figuring ME out, but that is my answer." I let the conversation go with him trying to process what I said. Again, during Christmas and over the New Year, I suggested he needed a break from all the pressures he was under, but to no avail.

One day in mid-December, as I was sitting in my office sewing the third of my chakra quilts, Conrad came and lay on the floor just to listen to the music and chat. I decided to throw the quilt I finished May 2018 on him, expecting the same reaction as usual. But to my surprise, he fell asleep. He looked so peaceful and content as he just laid there under the quilt, sleeping. I smiled and continued sewing, leaving him for a while to enjoy a rest.

Just before Christmas, Conrad decided to take me Christmas shopping at Athletes Foot. Seriously, I don't exercise, so this would be interesting. The first thing the shop assistant asked me was, "So what type of shoe do you like?" My reply—to my husband shaking his head—was, "See that little shoe shop on the other side of the shops?" I asked as I pointed out of the store. "I would like a nice little pair of flats in orange if I could." I laughed and laughed and laughed. Well that went down like a lead balloon. Conrad couldn't apologise to the poor guy enough, and he advised him of my bad sense of humour. I tried on several pair of shoes and decided on the most comfortable pair of sneakers, describing them as "F..ing kayaks!"

Christmas came and went, and this uneasy feeling got stronger and stronger. Far out!

What is it? I wondered. A little voice in my head replied, *You're not being true to yourself. You cannot hide any longer. There is a lightning bolt headed your way. Brace yourself!*

In my head I was already running as fast as I could, and I was starting to panic.

New Year's Day 2019

After weeks of torment in my head and this sickening feeling getting stronger and stronger, I decided to sit down with my husband and try to get him to see and hear me. The only way I knew how to do this was to finally step up, and after thirty years together, I said, "Things need to change. I cannot continue like this." I tried to tell him about the lightning bolt and the torment in my head, but he did not understand me. I was scared and told him that "I am stepping back to stay." I felt we needed a break and that I should look at finding a place to stay for a few months for us to work on things. I wanted to rent a four-bedroom house close to home, so we could have "date nights" and try and work on us. I didn't want to upset the family and felt if I got a four-bedroom place, it gave the kids an option to stay over as well. This hurt me, and the last thing I wanted to do was hurt my husband and my family, but I didn't know how else to plead my case.

Conrad's first comment was, "Fine. We will sell everything we worked for, and I will look for work in far north QLD." I told him that was his choice. We had very different points of view. Mine was to stay close to home with as little disruption as possible to the family and work things out. Conrad's was to sell everything and move to the other end of the state.

We were so different, and this was how our thirty years had been. He often commented that I had opposition defiance disorder. I used to laugh and respond with, "How do I oppose when I am the one who suggested in the first instance?"

This conversation was one of the hardest I have ever had to have. I didn't want to lose everything, but I certainly couldn't have it stay the way it was. I loved my husband, but we were no longer "in love." We had raised three beautiful young-adult children, had a lovely home and great jobs, but we had lost each other. My life was all work and work, and Conrad's was cricket and work. Don't get me wrong. I loved my husband's passion and desire to give to the community, and he did an amazing job at this. He was well respected and obtained hundreds of thousands of dollars for the community. He was very passionate about seeing local kids grow, and he fully supported this by coaching and captaining the youth team. But for me, there were so many nights when I sat alone at home, holding back the tears. You can have a million people around you and still be the loneliest. I tried to fill the void with poker machines (as noted in October 2017), and I could not go back to that space after finally getting back my family's trust. So I just worked harder each day, but I missed the emotion, I missed us, and I didn't know who I was. I gave him the following poem to try and explain how I felt.

My Place?

Some days I just sit
And stare into space.
I feel I don't fit
Or belong in this place.

The feelings I have
Deep down inside
Tumble and turn
And refuse to hide.

They are pushing me
Way out of my comfort zone
And are now having me question,
"Where is home?"

Every day I get up smiling
And run through the motion.
A mum, a wife, a support
But no one's there to share my emotion.

You can have a million people
Look you in the face
But still be sitting
Alone in a lonely space.

I'm getting tired
Of hiding behind a mask,
And being everyone's expectation
Is becoming a bigger task.

As the tears sneak up
And roll down my face,
I start to wonder,
Where is my place?

The universe is stepping in
And showing me what I must know.
But taking that step—
It's not easy to go.

To find an ear, a heart,
Even a cuddle is a mission,

Cos every time I reach out,
There seems to be a condition.

As the tears start to roll
Down my face once more,
I'm reaching out again
Before I walk through the door.

I've written you songs
And put my heart on my sleeve.
There's always been a reason
Not to leave.

But today I just sit
And stare into space.
The time is here.
I need to find my place.

It broke my heart knowing I had upset him, but for years, I had upset myself in not being me. It was getting harder every day to hide behind the "expected" mask. So much so, that I was having pains in the lower chest and abdomen, I wasn't sleeping, and I could feel my energy levels depleting daily. That was so not me. For one of the very first times, I actually saw a tear come to his eyes, and this hurt me even more. We have always tried to have a very open family relationship, and more so after our daughter's anorexia. The therapy I found for her was family-based cognitive, and communication was one of the biggest factors in her growth and healing journey. We decided to speak to the kids about where we were in life and advised them, "Mum and Dad are trying to sort a few things, and if you see us off talking or processing things, do not worry. We are working hard to find a resolution."

The Calm before the Storm

On January 3, 2019, we both returned to work for another year. But for both of us, a heavy load sat on our shoulders. We never argued or fought, but over the previous few days, there had certainly been a strain. Conrad was trying to figure out who caused these changes in me; he felt there was a third party. He started to question events back to October. He blamed my association with Lorna and then my Gold Coast course. He was sure that Lorna had an ulterior motive and was the reason for this. I tried to reassure him that was not the case, and the universe sent these people to me to support me in whatever journey I had coming up. I just didn't know yet what that was, but the lightning bolt was still very much in my mind.

When I got to work and opened my emails, I had received several from my husband doing his research on me and my way of thinking. I smiled and thought it was beautiful that he was finally listening. Conrad is very logical and didn't understand me or nontangible things. So when I talked about energies or metaphysical subjects to him, it was all rubbish, and I was off with the "fairies." I often said, "It's a nicer place, and they don't judge me!"

To open an email and find the subject was based on my "non-logic" topic told me he was out of his comfort zone and really making an effort. He had googled "empath" and sent me several links to try to show me how much he was learning. That night as we lay in bed, he started to ask me questions about what I felt were his underlying emotions and patterns that were not productive for him and, more so, about our relationship. I told him upfront our biggest issue was his control. I was expecting backlash, but to his credit, he listened and asked more questions. He asked me where I thought it came from. My reply was, "We have been together for over thirty years, and during that whole time, there are only three things I know about your childhood, and one of the most traumatic events was losing a house in a fire at an early age. What if at that time your conscious mind made the decision to never not have control again? Do you suppose this could have been a foundation for decisions made after that trauma that is now your basis in life?" I gave him several examples of situations along our journey that were very much based on control. These were not isolated to just me. There were situations at work, sport, with friends, and more. Each of these lessons, as I described them to him, were getting bigger and bigger, and I felt he still wasn't learning in his life path.

I explained that you need to acknowledge an emotion to be able to let it go. If you don't—if you suppress it—it comes out as ailments in your body. You don't need to go back and play in the trauma (e.g., a house fire) that caused the emotion (control), but if you acknowledge the emotion, you can let it go.

The very next day I noticed a lighter side of Conrad, and so did the kids. He actually had them in the backyard helping him garden while I got a sleep in. He usually had the blinds pulled back and was telling me it was the best time of day, and I had to get up. When I walked out to the yard and questioned the kids about this, they were surprised that Dad had actually asked them to help him for half an hour—and without the usual delegation on how to help. This was a first and was noted by the kids as well.

Over the next two weeks, I looked forward to the challenges Conrad found for me and the questions that he posed for me to give him my thought process on. He purchased books to read and surprised me several times with an article or book he had ordered about empaths, sabotage monkeys, and metaphysics. Each night we sat chatting in bed for hours about the discoveries he made during the day. I had opened something in him that he had never experienced on many levels. On several occasions, he apologised for holding me back and not taking the time to understand me and my alternate way of thinking. He often commented that I needed to follow this path and how I had stimulated something in his mind that was previously lacking. When he realised I had locked in my first workshop for January 21, he was the driving force in having me start to set up my web page (currently on hold) and a Facebook page (Alternate Life Coach). He came home each day straight from work and had an excitement about him. He often mentioned he didn't want to go back out to cricket but had to due to his commitment. Then he would reluctantly leave to fulfil that commitment.

We both started to look at where we could improve ourselves, and part of my discovery in those few weeks was my own shortfall in never finishing a project. For twenty-five years I would get something 95 per cent finished, and whether it be curtains for the house, or clothes, I never actually finished a project. Conrad agreed with me, and when he challenged me on where this came from, I went within. I realised after going back through my mind that it went back to when I got married. I spent eighteen months making my dress and the bridesmaids' dresses. My mother-in-law is a seamstress, and I was never taught to sew, so I tried to prove my worth to her by making all the dresses. A week out from the wedding, I found out that my sister-in-law had taken the dress I made for her to wear to her mother to have it "fixed" as I didn't have the seams lined up. This, to me, meant I failed and was something I had taken on at the time as an emotion of a failure without even realising it. It was at that point I understood where my unfinished tasks came from. I felt that if a project I had been working on was never completed, I always had an excuse if it fell short to anyone because I could say it wasn't finished.

When I explained this to Conrad, he took it in and suggested I could be right. He wanted to help me push through my bad habit and put 100 per cent into finishing the workshop set for January 21. He actually got excited in helping me and gave me ideas and feedback. These nightly conversations and daily challenges with Conrad had us communicating like we had never before. And for both of us, it was exciting and brought us closer together. For the first time in thirty years, I could actually express what thoughts were running in my head. I know his eyes rolled and he thought, *She has lost it*, but credit to him, he actually listened and got a lot from our deep conversations each night, as did I.

I remember about a week into January, I woke up with an unexplainable depleted energy level. This was very much unlike me and was concerning at the time. When I mentioned this to Conrad, he was the absolute opposite and said for some reason, he had this beautiful burst of energy in his heart space and was loving this new energy. When I asked him how he had slept, he surprised me with, "I didn't. I sat and watched you all night and just rubbed your back." Hmm, that almost sounded wrong, but I quickly realised he had unintentionally drawn my energy from me while I slept. I had learned over the years to protect my energy levels and not get drained when I walked into a room. But when I was asleep and safe in bed, I never thought this was possible. It was a beautiful and valuable lesson learned for an empath!

For the next few days, it took all I could muster to regain the energy I had expelled. My family started to express its concerns at my lethargy and wanted me to go to the doctor to get medication. I had hit rock bottom with my energy levels and could hardly think or move. My family was about to hit panic mode and have it addressed without my approval. I pleaded for them to give me a few days. I knew I had the tools, but I had not even thought to use them. I told them if they wanted to help me, all they needed to do was to run me a bath and I would fix this. I grabbed my Clary Sage (essential oil) and an armful of crystals, ran a big bubble bath, and set an intention grid with my crystals at the end of the bath. When I had finished laying out the crystal grid, I noticed my family looking at me with much interest. Conrad said he had never seen me look so content and at peace as I was just playing with the crystals. I told him, "This is me. This is how I heal and how I get my peace and strength." It was nice to just do something without fear of judgement or laughter.

The first two weeks of January had seen so much progress and opening up for both Conrad and me that it was what I had been craving for the last thirty years. He suggested we renew our wedding vows in August for our twenty-fifth wedding anniversary and asked me to take him to Bali, where my journey really started. It blew me away as Conrad was so against me going there back in 2017. He had never entertained the idea of leaving the country, and to suggest it was a first. Annually, I tried to arrange a surprise weekend away to a destination we had never visited. I had planned on taking him to Adelaide for the weekend of February 3 to watch the Adelaide Strikers play the Brisbane Heat in our much-loved 20/20 Big Bash. But something inside me held back on booking flights and accommodations. I still had this lightning bolt above me, and it was getting stronger and stronger in my mind.

On Saturday, January 12, I got a phone call from Conrad saying he had an intense pain in his lower chest and was short of breath. He had just scored sixty-two runs in his cricket batting stance, and it was a hot day. He put the pain down to heat exhaustion, but several of his friends told him to go to the hospital because it was his heart. For five days he refused to accept that he needed help. He thought he had a pinched nerve and went to the chiropractor and for a massage. No matter how many times we told him to go to the hospital or doctor, he outright refused. On January 15, he asked me for an aspirin, which was very unusual as we don't have them in the house, and aspirin is a blood thinner. Conrad, out of the blue, on January 16 said he felt his grandmother was "around"; she passed in the 1990s. Again, this was very odd for him.

January 17 came, and we both headed off to work like any other day. After he got off work, Conrad went to cricket to coach the boys and sort the weekend's team for the next round of fixtures. I called him around five o'clock to see how he was feeling, and he still felt unwell. I finished work at 7:15 and called into the cricket fields on the way home to help finalise the barbecue and help clean up after training, as I sometimes did. When I arrived, Conrad looked pale and very unwell. He indicated he had a severe pain in his shoulders. I told him I would take him to the hospital, but he refused as he needed to finalise the team selection. I pushed for him to put himself first, and the team could sort the final tasks for the night. I asked our eldest son to drive Conrad's car home, and I took Conrad in my car.

We walked in the door at 8:05 on Thursday, January 17, 2019. I went to the bathroom, and Conrad went to the fridge to steal a swig of milk.

Batten Down
the Hatches:
The Storm Hits

As I walked out of the bathroom, I heard my son Brodie yell for me. I ran to the kitchen to see Conrad slide down the cupboard with my son trying to support him on his way down. Our whole world turned upside down as he hit the ground. I yelled for my daughter to call an ambulance as Brodie and I turned Conrad on his side. The whole time he was gasping for air and bringing up the milk that he had just ingested. What was left of the three litres of milk hit the ground and spewed from the bottle. I ran for the neighbour, who is a registered nurse. She and her son came in minutes and started CPR on him. The entire time they worked on him, our daughter was on the phone with the paramedics, relaying information. Brodie kept his throat clear by holding the neck and head with slight pressure on the throat to ensure the airways were open to the best ability, and every so often, Conrad would gasp for air. I kept reassuring him that we were right beside him, and the paramedics were on their way. I held his hand, and when I looked into his eyes, he was not there. I felt he had left his body. His pupils were very small, and there was nothing—just blue eyes seeing nothing.

My neighbour and her son took turns of pumping my husband's chest to keep him alive while Brodie tried and to keep his airways clear. The paramedics arrived fifteen to twenty minutes later and took over from my exhausted neighbour and her son. The paramedics pushed us outside to allow them to do what was needed to get him stable, and hopefully, to hospital for help. Our neighbour's son formed a circle with me and our three kids, and prayed with all we had. I looked up and in my mind's eye saw my dad, who passed in 1996, and Conrad's grandparents, who had also passed. I told them, "You send him back to us now! He needs to look after your grandchildren, and we need him. I can't do this on my own." I then called Conrad's parents on the mobile to tell them what happened. They are in their seventies, and at least a two-and-a-half hour drive away.

I heard the paramedics in the background, but nothing made sense. "Tube him. Get this monitor on him. We need to stabilise him. We cannot move him. Charge." The next forty-five minutes they worked on him to get him stable enough to put him in one of the three ambulances waiting in front of our house. I am not sure at what point I went into autopilot, but without my neighbours—in particular the nurse and her calm head—I am not sure how I would have coped.

As the ambulance headed towards the hospital, our neighbour drove me and the kids, while her son followed in their car to bring her home. The whole time she tried to reassure us but also advise us of the seriousness of what happened. When we arrived at the hospital, the paramedics were out in the emergency bay and told us that Conrad had another turn on the way to hospital. They had charged him four times just to get him to the emergency department. They advised us that things did not look good.

The kids and I were left in the waiting room for what seemed to be an eternity before a nurse came to take us up to the intensive care unit (ICU). They had taken Conrad into surgery to try and see what the problem was. We were advised he had a large blood clot in one of the main arteries, and they had no way to remove it. He was put on life support and taken to ICU. The doctors did not give us a favourable prognosis. He was recorded as not having oxygen to the brain for forty-five minutes and damage to the heart's left ventricle chamber. The next forty-eight hours would determine whether he lived.

Sitting in the waiting room for hours, the mind tends to run its own race and come up with many ideas. As previously noted, I feel that any internal illness is linked to an emotion. If you are hit by a car, say, there is a logical and tangible reason for an illness. But if the internal illness doesn't have a logical reason, then I look for the emotional possibility. I started to ask, "What life lesson do we need to learn and acknowledge in this situation?" So based on my theory of patterns and repeat behaviours, I came up with the following.

> Me: I can't change the situation that put Conrad in the ICU, but what can I do to learn from this situation? *Be true to yourself and trust your inner guidance.*

> Conrad: Your whole life you have had control of situations, and now, every bit of control has been taken from you to the point of not being able to do anything, including breathing.

Empaths tend to feel other people's energies, so a hospital is one of the most draining places to be. The first time I got to see my husband lying in the bed, it was confronting. I had never been in an ICU, and had been fortunate enough, until then, not to have a loved one in such a serious condition. He had tubes and machines hooked up to every part of his body. And the noise of those machines I will never forget. I touched his arm and closed my eyes. I saw in my mind's eye my husband inside a vault and in a panicked state. The vision kept playing in my mind. Then the vision changed to a large hedged labyrinth. And again, Conrad was in a panic, trying to get out of it. I felt his energy in a fight-or-flight state. I felt and knew he was in there. I truly believed I just had to find him the combination to get out. The panic in him was *real*. In my mind, he was thrashing and very distressed. But when I looked at his body, he was motionless and on life support. I have never felt such a strong emotion and a state of fear in anyone as I did at that moment in Conrad. I had to find a way to get him the tools to fight. I knew he was in there.

When I finally had a chance to stop and process what happened, I looked to find a reason for Conrad's cardiac arrest and what positive could come from such a dire situation. I know in scientific studies the brain has much unknown surrounding it and what it is capable of. I started to wonder if the brain could have somehow shut itself down, no different than what a computer would do if a power surge were to hit it. The computer's hard drive knows to shut down to protect the software, so why can't the brain's subconscious mind have known this was coming and gone into "protection mode" before the conscious mind said, "Fix the problem"? When I mentioned this to the doctors, I was dismissed. I insisted that we didn't know enough about the brain to say what it is or isn't capable of doing. The doctor told me there was no way this could have happened, and in his words, "You need a miracle. Of a hundred people who suffer this injury, ninety do not get up off the floor. Of the remaining ten, one *may* walk again. The rest vary through to brain dead and vegetable state."

I acknowledged his comment and respectfully replied, "I just need a higher vibrational frequency. I will not give up, Dr 1." This got a very odd look.

We need foundations that are strong if we are going to hit rough weather. I needed to ensure I had unconditional support around me to keep me balanced. I looked to the sky and asked for some guidance on who would be the right person/s for me in this journey. My dad, who passed away in 1996, immediately came through along with a vision of his best friend from thirty years ago, Peter, and his wife, Lesley. The kids and I affectionately call them Uncle Petie and Aunty Lee Lee. Aunty Lee Lee has a very big toolbox when it comes to therapy and alternate advise. She is a counsellor, a hypnotherapist, and a clairvoyant, to name a few of her gifts. When I called them and asked if they could help with my spiritual support, they did not hesitate to help us in any way they could. I called Lorna to help keep my chatter monkeys in check if they were to start with their destructive talk in my mind. We all have them, and I am very mindful of how the internal chatter can throw us in a spin pretty quickly. Leon also offered to help in any way he could. I asked for him to be available for my logical support. I knew he had an extensive career with the Australian forces, and he had encountered several situations of people in cardiac arrest or similar medical events. At times, he was very forthcoming with his reality of how dire the situation was. He kept me balanced with his logic when I ran on too much emotion. Each evening on my way home from the hospital, he would call and check on Conrad, me, and the kids. He listened to my crazy talk and gave me insight into his experiences with this type of trauma, especially in the earlier days. He also mentioned that he was an acquaintance of the paramedic who initially assisted with Conrad, and he had told Leon that on the evening he went down, something made them go the extra time and well above the normal process for a cardiac arrest. It was comforting to know he knew someone who worked on Conrad that night. The above people, knowing I could be totally raw and honest in my discussions with these them, gave me a go-to when I struggled to process thoughts on my own.

My brother was quick to make sure we had money and a fuel card to take off some of the financial pressure that we would soon endure. Hospital parking is a killer! My mum and her husband arrived from Newcastle in the first few days to make sure the kids and I had a meal cooked and a clean house to come home to each evening. For this I will be forever grateful. Conrad's family had their own emotions to deal with in this as it was their son and brother. And I had to focus on Conrad, the kids, and myself. Everyone had their own beliefs about what would happen and shared stories of their experiences. But I stood firm in my belief system, and this didn't always align with others. As previously stated, my thinking can be very different from that of others, and for me that works. I don't try to force my thoughts on other people, but in this instance, I needed to come back to centre and stay strong in my convictions. The eye-rolling and huffing when I spoke to people alerted me pretty quickly with whom I could share my thoughts openly. And I was okay with that.

It did, however, have me pull within and minimised the circle around me as the comments at times were harsh. I was advised after a few weeks that a request was made in that first week to ask for me to "pull my head in, and stop going down this path, otherwise legal advice would need to be sought. It was not fair to prolong the inevitable and cause more pain and that Conrad would not want this." When I heard this statement, I felt sick, and I was angry. It also had me withdraw further as I didn't know whom I could trust.

The first forty-eight hours were a blur. We spent every waking hour at the hospital and beside Conrad. While sitting in the waiting room, I decided to write a poem each day for me to read to him; this continued every day. I knew he was in there, and he would hear me on a subconscious level. He just couldn't respond on a conscious level. I made a genuine effort at every point not to not have negative energy around him or allow him to see me cry. I always redirected anyone from the room who was too upset as I felt Conrad would feel this. The doctors were ruthless in their conversations with me. I often pulled them up or had them take the conversation outside. On more than three occasions I had a doctor actually lean directly over Conrad, with his finger pointed at me and telling me that I had a, "brain-dead husband who would be a vegetable, and Conrad wouldn't want his young family to have this burden." And based on this doctor's medical experience, the right thing to do was turn off the life support machines. I pulled him up often on the way he spoke and the topic of discussion. I told him several times that I wasn't stupid and could read between the lines and to cease his line of conversation immediately in Conrad's presence. His reply was often that Conrad needed to hear what he was saying. I disagreed and stopped the conversation whenever I felt he was pushing in a negative direction. Or I would walk out of the room to have him converse with me outside.

Tests on Conrad's brain and heart were inconclusive, and his response, or lack thereof, was their "fact or logic" to say he was brain-dead. I did not accept this. The first few days, the doctors advised they would be respectful of the family and give us time to grieve and process the loss we were about to experience. But they told me I needed to be aware of the costs and the intensity involved in the staffing to support such a high need, especially one who would not have a favourable outcome at any point.

The first day after Conrad's cardiac arrest, I sat the kids down to see how they were in all this and to check in. They understood the severity of the situation, but I told them I could not turn off their dad's life support until I was 100 per cent confident that I had done all I thought possible, no matter how nonlogical or what people might not understand. I would not make a decision until I had exhausted all I thought may be available to give him the tools to fight. I told them what I felt about their dad when I first saw him, as in the vault, but I also told them the doctor I did the workshop with in October (Dr Alt) had also come through, and I needed to see if she could help on an energy level. I reassured them this was not our doing, and that Conrad had to choose whether he would stay. It was a hard road for him to fight, and he may not make it through, but it was his choice. All we could do was fully support him and show him how much we loved him by being there, talking to him, playing music, and always staying positive.

The kids understood my need in this and told me to do whatever I felt necessary to ensure their dad had a chance, no matter how out there it was. They would support me in my decision. They fully understood this might not be acceptable to other family members as they were very logical in their thought processes. But our kids assured me they supported me no matter what. That evening I sent a group text to family and friends, letting them know what happened and advised them that I would do my best to send an update each day.

On the second day that Conrad was on life support, I got a phone call from Aunty Lee Lee. She was a little overwhelmed as she had a message from my dad. He told her that I needed, "to get that quilt I made to Conrad immediately as this was his quilt, and he needed it for his healing." Aunty Lee Lee had not heard about or seen my quilt but could see a dominant orange in her mind and asked me if I knew what this meant. I laughed and said yes. I explained to her the quilt I finished making on Mother's Day 2018, and yes, its dominant colour was orange. She told me that Dad was adamant, and she didn't fancy him turning up again while she was in the shower to pass on messages. We both laughed. I told Chantelle what the phone call was, and we drove home to get the quilt.

When I got back to the ICU and placed the quilt on Conrad, I told him about my conversation with Aunty Lee Lee. I felt his energy settle and soften. I told him the quilt was his direct line to me twenty-four hours a day, and even if I wasn't beside him, the quilt would be with him. I explained to him how I felt the universe had given me the right people in this and how I had spoken to the kids about going to the Gold Coast, hoping to see the doctor there to help him energetically. I told him I would do all I could to help him. It was at this point I saw a tear roll down his cheek. When I asked the nurse about this, she advised it was the drops they had administered to try keep his eyes moist, but to me, it was a tear.

Day 2 in ICU—Conrad with His "Healing Quilt"

Day 2 also saw him trying to cough. I tuned into him and felt heavy in the chest. I told the doctors I felt he was getting a chest infection. They told me it was a residual effect of cardiac arrest and normal for fluid to develop in the lungs. It was another complication I needed to be mindful of. This didn't sit right with me, and again, I told them I would like to have this further investigated. Conrad is prone to chest infections, and they come on very quickly. He can go to bed in the evening and by morning needs Ventolin and antibiotics. I asked them to do a test and to note this history on file. I also queried his weight-to-medicine ratio as I overheard them talk about his current weight, and to me, this was almost twenty kilos lighter than his actual weight. I felt this had an impact on the amount of medicine he needed. This was finally adjusted, but only after I pushed the point several times. Later that day, the coughing got worse, and again I pushed the doctors to put him put on medication and run some tests. This time they did.

On day 3 he was moved to another unit within the ICU and to a room of his own. The doctors told us they had done this to give our family privacy in the current situation. Again the doctor started to discuss how dire the situation was. I pulled the doctor outside the room and confirmed I understood the severity of what he was saying and could read between the lines. I also knew they had budgets and KPIs to meet, but I was not giving up on my husband. He was in there, and I just needed to give him the opportunity to prove it. The doctor was again quite ruthless in his comments about my husband and the situation.

I called Lorna to tell her I was hoping to get an appointment with her doctor on the Gold Coast as she had come through quite strong in my mind on the first day Conrad went down. The doctor is generally booked out weeks in advance. It turned out Lorna had an appointment with her the following Thursday and was willing to give me this appointment if I needed it. Hell yeah!

I sat with Conrad as much as I could but also had to share the time with his family and our children. We were only allowed two at a time in his cubicle, and this made it hard when there were six to eight people in the waiting room to see him at any time. When I did sit with Conrad, I told him on more than one occasion that all he needed to do was to let go of trying to control the situation and trust those around him. He had to save all his strength to fight when the need arose. His only task was to focus on his breathing. This was written on a board beside his bed with a note from me requesting the nurses repeat this to him as often as possible in the way of affirmations. I had taken a few family photos to be put beside his bed, along with a few crystals that resonated with me. I have not had a script for over twenty years and have a very strong belief that the earth provides us with a lot of natural options for healing. So first and foremost, if I am unwell, I go to my essential oils and crystals for their healing properties. This is not everyone's cup of tea, but it works for me. I meditated on what crystals I wanted to place in his room and was guided to a beautiful amethyst crystal tree. Amethyst helps one relax and is a very calming crystal. It is also a powerful and protective stone. I was also drawn to a piece of rose quartz (for love) and lapis lazuli (encourages self-awareness). And finally, a nice piece of clear quartz, said to be the master of all healing crystals. It also amplifies the properties of all other crystals that sit with it.

Day 4 the ICU doctor told me this was a "marathon." Okay, I don't exercise, but I will take on the challenge with the new sneakers that I got for Christmas. Conrad got the lecture on this one while lying in the hospital bed. He knew! I had to admit, though, the sneakers were comfortable. The following day I had them on with the brightest yoga pants I could find along with the brightest dress. It didn't match. It was an unusual sight but certainly lifted my spirits when I turned up to the ICU. The nurses laughed with me as I described my attire to Conrad.

On day 5, this daily update was sent out to family and friends.

Hi All Group Text

Tuesday update

Gotta be honest, yesterday I hit a wall hard, but my motto has always been, "I have roots that go deep into the ground, and no matter how bad I feel getting into bed, every morning that I get up is another day. My roots won't let me down.

So with that and my bad humour, I threw on the sneakers (after a bit of a sookie moment) and my psychedelic yoga pants, along with the brightest dress I could find, to step out in style. (Ummm, not sure if that is what you would call it. It was tacky. lol.)

The doctor we had today was lovely and explained a little more. He is still "nonresponsive," but they will be putting a hole in his throat (not sure on doctor term but can guarantee not what I called it) and put the tube in there to make it a little more comfortable for him.

Friday they are going to do an MRI, and Monday hoping to have an update.

So I am picking the positive in this. They are still progressing, and he is not going backwards.

Thank you for reading and caring.

If you want to go further, I write a poem every day, and today's is as follows:

Hey, Bub,
you are still my loving hub.
I got my sneakers on today
to tackle what you throw my way.
We had a good laugh at the shoe store.
But I had no idea what these sneakers were for.
With bright yoga pants on
and playing in my heart a sad song,
I'll put a big girl smile on my face.
You know I don't exercise, but I'm in for your race.
Luv you moon and back!
You got this, babe.

Toward the end of the first week, Conrad was taken for further tests on his brain to try and ascertain the damage done due to lack of oxygen. While he was in having the MRI, I took the opportunity to grab his quilt and take it outside to "charge it." It was a beautiful sunny day, and as I sat on the grass outside with crystals (selinite to help with bringing light from higher realms, rose quartz for love, and clear quartz to amplify) on the quilt and a playlist we had created for Conrad playing in the background, I looked up to the sky and asked for whatever my guides needed and what Conrad's higher-self needed to be put into this quilt and for them to use me as the channel. Immediately images started to flow through me. I saw images of us as teenagers, our wedding day, the day we found out we were pregnant with our first child (after seven years of trying), and the birth of each of our kids. The memories just flowed and flowed. Initially, I could see the images and knew what they were. But after the first few seconds, I felt them downloading at such a fast pace that I no longer saw them, but I felt the energy as it passed through me and the memories went into the quilt. This quilt had everything I could possibly think of to give him support. I took it back to the ICU when he returned from his MRI and told the nurses it was not to leave his bed. I didn't care if it just touched his little toe, but it was to remain with him at all times.

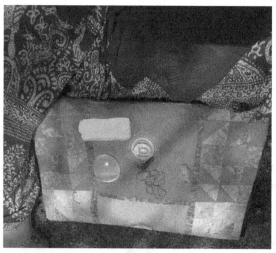

Charging and Downloading into Conrad's Quilt

Each day I continued to write him a poem and read it to him. During this whole journey, I talked to Conrad and told him what I was going to do and what I had done. He couldn't argue or disagree; he had to listen. I had a captured audience. When I took the quilt back to him, I got to spend a little uninterrupted time with him. I rested on his arm while listening to the playlist the kids and I created for him and just sang softly to him. I knew he heard and felt us there. I picked this up in his energy on any day.

I watched him closely and picked up on so much about how he was feeling or if there were things the nurses needed to be advised about. This was very obvious after about a week in and after another coughing fit. The nurses had to suction his mouth out several times an hour. I watched them do this, and each time I got a pain in my mouth. I felt this was linked to Conrad, so I walked around to his side and saw his forehead move in a pained expression and his bottom lip quiver. When I told the nurses, "Stop it. You are hurting him," they assured me he couldn't feel it as he was heavily sedated, and because he was nonresponsive, he couldn't react. Conrad is prone to mouth ulcers and having the tube down his throat, along with the constant coughing, I could guarantee his oesophagus and mouth were covered in ulcers. When the nurse checked the side of his tongue and his cheeks, she saw they were ulcerated. As she cleaned his mouth the next time, I pointed out the pained look on his forehead and quivering lip. Many studies have been done on facial expressions and the emotions they relate to. There are seven micro-expressions that cannot be hidden. No matter how you try, they show in your face and eyes. The nurse saw the expressions I pointed out and immediately took more care. This alone seemed to reduce the impact on him, but his mouth was still very sore, and again I saw a tear roll down his face. I asked her to make note for future cleans and to let the other

43

nurses know to be more careful. I cringed while watching the process each time. I held his hand and assured him the nurses were doing their best to reduce the pain. It broke my heart each time I saw the bottom lip quivering, and it bought a tear to my eyes every clean.

On Thursday, January 21, I drove to the Gold Coast with much excitement to see Dr Alt. I had hope that she may be able to give me some guidance and direction in Conrad's healing. As an energetic doctor, she tunes in to a person's subconscious and higher being. This can also be done via a willing surrogate—very much out there, I know—and I was more than willing to try anything to support his healing.

For months prior to Conrad going down, I had been researching muscle testing and tuning in to the subconscious mind. It had piqued an interest in me and something I started to investigate further. Our subconscious minds cannot lie, and based on muscle testing and proven medical studies, you can get answers about what our bodies need by using simple body movements, providing our conscious minds does not override the subconscious. As humans, we have free will, the ability to make choices, which we do on a conscious level every day. It is our personalities or egos that choose what path we take. We often have a gut feeling not to do something, and this is our inner guidance trying to direct us on a path. This is not always supported by our egos or what we want at that time, and no matter how the gut feeling tries to have us go one way, we choose the other only to find out later it may not be the right choice. Our subconscious knows what is right for our bodies at all times. And if you know how to tune in to this, you will get the right answers.

The first thing the Dr Alt said was, "He is not in his body." He had passed four times, and there was no way he could heal if he was not present. She also noted several times to me this was his journey and choice as to whether he stayed or left this earth, and the kids and I needed to respect that and not take that burden on. She did some energetic healing on him by tuning in to his subconscious, using me as a surrogate. She also worked on his fight or flight. As a qualified naturopath, she made sure that I was okay by checking my lymphatic system, adrenal gland, and thyroid and administered a treatment for me.

During my appointment, I ran past her the thoughts I had on the brain and if it could put itself into protection mode before damage was done. Her reply was comforting, and I was grateful I didn't get the "look." She commented that we don't know enough about the brain to say what it is capable of. Scientists and medics only know a small percentage of the brain's abilities, so anything is possible. I left feeling I had made the right choice in seeing her, if for nothing else but to give me hope. I never have expectations on anything in life as you tend to be disappointed if the outcome is not as you hoped. I always go into a situation with an open mind and take one step at a time. I made another appointment for the following week if a cancellation arose.

Each day the doctors discussed Conrad's nonresponsive behaviour and told us to let him go. I refused to give in. The results from his MRI had come back with no indication of brain damage, but the doctors told me this was common, and we were to base his prognosis and future outcome on his behaviour at that time, which was nothing. Every day the doctors pulled me aside. One doctor stated on a regular basis that five days in the ICU was pretty much the time they like to have before moving them to a ward. He started to discuss the best options for us as a family to let him go. He tried to comfort me that the kids would not have to see their dad suffer, and they would ensure that his death certificate would indicate infection. He would make certain Conrad would be on minimal machines, and a specialist would be in another closed room to monitor him and maintain his pain levels. I took a deep breath and challenged his to-date reports about the MRI and CT scans that were done. If they were inconclusive, how could they know where Conrad would or wouldn't get better? I looked at the doctor and adamantly stated, "I'm not going away, Dr 1. I will not give up!"

The doctors kept telling me we had to wait and see, and there wasn't much more they could advise. I repeatedly asked for more testing. The doctors must have finally gotten sick of my constant nagging and ordered a brain specialist from another hospital to evaluate Conrad. A week later, an EEG was done and again the results were inconclusive as they had received what they called "scattered signals." A report was done based on professional opinion and patient history of similar health patterns. The report noted that he had severe brain damage based on his current behaviours and daily assessments of not responding. It was noted that due to lack of oxygen to the brain for forty-five minutes, he had sustained a hypoxic brain injury. And based on this information, he would not have a quality of life. Again, I felt this was not evidence enough to say this would be his final progress. To me, the report was based on assumptions. As the reports scans were shown to me, Dr 1 often pointed out that it was common for these reports to be inconclusive, and in his experience, Conrad would not have a quality of life. Another round of "Would he want this? You are a young family, this is what you have got," as he pointed at Conrad. Again I smiled and give him the same reply, "I am not going away, Dr 1. My husband is still in there."

During the first week, I also contacted Karen, a former work colleague of both Conrad and mine. Karen is very intuitive and has her own business in crystals, Reiki, and massage. She was very compassionate about our situation and repeatedly told me this was Conrad's journey, and the kids and I had to accept that. She touched base every few days to see how we were travelling and give insight to what had been guided to her at the time, if she felt it necessary. I remember her telling me that Conrad would become my biggest guide if he chose to leave this earth. And if he stayed, he would become one of my biggest supporters and help me make a difference in the logic that people needed when it came to understanding this journey.

I remember receiving a text message from Karen in the first week or two at about 5 a.m. stating, "Received the message, it's time to put scolecite around Conrad. Couldn't sleep as I kept hearing it. I haven't worked with it much as it's a hard one to find. Sorry about the ungodly hour."

I jumped out of bed to go to my room where I keep all my crystal. The ever so beautiful scolecite was looking straight at me. I replied to Karen with a photo, "Noooooooo way. For some reason (Seriously, I am not asking.) I had to buy this a few months back. I had never heard of it. Here goes. Thank you, honey." Thinking back to when I purchased the crystal, I was drawn to it when I went to the Gold Coast for my workshop the previous October. I jumped online to see what Scolicite's healing properties and smiled as it is one of the higher vibrational crystals. It is a strong stone to aid communication, especially with spirit. It is a stone that resonates with the chakras from the heart up. It facilitates deep inner peace and spiritual transformation. The next morning the crystal was the first thing put into the car, along with an oil mix I made to massage his feet.

I often look up healing properties of crystals and essential oils to see what I can learn. It was interesting to me that some oils have more oxygenating properties than others and help the brain. I made up several blends to be used for Conrad in both his foot massages early on and later on his head. I ensured they were safe to use and didn't have other affects, such as lowering the blood pressure or thinning the blood. I do not use oils unless they are safe to do so. I do research on this. In some instances, I checked with Conrad's doctor at the time, those who were more open to their use.

Essentials oils have the unique ability to penetrate cell membranes and diffuse throughout the blood and tissues very quickly. They are one of the only molecules small enough to cross the brain–blood barrier, where medication may not have the ability to directly access the limbic system or emotional seat of the brain.

Conrad constantly struggled with high temperatures and fighting off infections. It was hard to see him lying on an ice bed shivering. The doctors advised us that the hypothalamus (the body's natural thermostat) regulated his temperature control, and his body had shut down to the extent of this not even working. The normal body temperature is about 36 degrees Celsius (98.6 Fahrenheit). Once it reaches above 38 degrees Celsius (100.4 Fahrenheit), it increases the risk of seizures. Conrad would drop in temperature to 36 degrees, but if the ice bed got turned off, his temp would peak close to 40 degrees Celsius (104 degrees Fahrenheit) in such a short time. Panadol was administered regularly. Daily they tried to bring him out of a coma, but he would start shivering uncontrollably, which caused his temp to rise again. It was a vicious cycle that was on repeat daily for the first few weeks. As I sat with him late one afternoon, only fifteen minutes before I was about to head home, I got an uneasy feeling and started to watch him closer. The nurses took his observations every half hour and had only just documented them in his medical chart. I asked a nurse to check them again. She advised they were due again in fifteen minutes. Within five minutes, I felt his body temperature rise quickly, and his forehead started to get very clammy. When I pointed this out to the nurse, she took his temperature again, and it was nearly 40 degrees Celsius (104 degrees Fahrenheit). This had the nurses racing to get ice blankets under his armpits and groin area to bring it down as quickly as possible. The quick spike in his temperature raised concerns and had him being monitored even closer. I cannot fault the nurses and their dedication to his situation.

Another week down, and after a cancellation, I went to the Gold Coast to visit my energy doctor. This week her focus was on his fight or flight and his body's "assemblage point." The human body has energy fields no different from our earth's. Each of these assemblage points needs to be aligned for the body to function in harmony and to repair itself. No different than a car being tuned up. If it is out of sync, it will run rough or not work at all. Our body is no different.

I was given the task of a meditation to do twice a day to help Conrad stay stable in his energy and assemblage point (again, way out there) for the next two weeks. The music made me feel quit sick each time I listened to it, but I was determined to do whatever I felt guided towards, and there was no harm in trying a meditation for half an hour a day. During the morning and night meditations, I tuned in to Conrad and visualised his energy field and body, and I locked in each of his energy points. Being Reiki-trained myself, I also did distance healing for him.

For the following two weeks, I battled daily with the doctors not to turn off his life support machines and to keep him as stable as possible in the ICU. Daily, Conrad battled very high temperatures, several infections, and constant involuntary movements. The doctors were sure he was having seizures but couldn't say what or where they were coming from. To say he kept them guessing is an understatement. He defied all medical logic to date, and I had no doubt he would continue to do so.

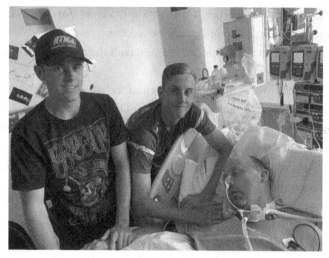

Conrad and Our Boys—Week 2 in the ICU

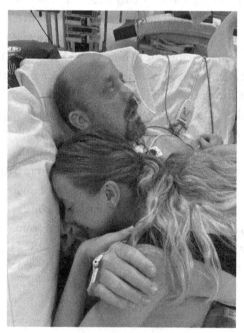

Always Dad's Girl

Two and a half weeks and several infections later, and with tubes in every port in Conrad's body, it was getting hard. The smell that hit me after one of his tubes had been left in place for days almost made me want to throw up. When I asked Dr 1 what it was and why they couldn't change the tube to remove his body waste, the doctor responded, "He is a decomposing body." WTF? My quick reply was, "My husband is not dead. He is *not* a decomposing body!" Dr 1 tried to get me to agree to a DNR (do not resuscitate) order if Conrad had another cardiac arrest. I told him I would not sign as I felt without a doubt he would "coincidentally" have another turn within a short time after. The doctor was horrified and said there was no way that would happen, but I would not relent to their request. They were to resus if needed. They were to do everything in their power to keep him alive. If he were to have another cardiac arrest and have further damage to his heart, I would reassess at that time.

The doctor then went on his usual rant. The next round started with him on, "your husband's quality of life, he wouldn't want this, this is not right," to my continued retorts of, "He's still here, Dr 1. You're surprised aren't you, Doctor. I'm not going away Dr 1."

It was getting harder each day to defend my actions in keeping him alive and on the machines to both doctors and family. I referred previously to Conrad having to let go of control and to trust those around him. This offended some people to the point of them releasing their frustration on me in a public place. I was yelled at and told, "He doesn't have control," and that I got to do whatever I wanted. After all, I had gone to Bali and wasted all our money on poker machines. They had their perceptions about events in our married life that they felt needed to be expressed. Over the first few days, our daughter had opened up to others and mentioned that Conrad and I had been going through a rough patch prior to Christmas. This had obviously been discussed, unbeknown to me at the time. People made assumptions about our marriage and not asked me at any point what the situation was. Though that upset me, it was the least of my concerns. I had no chance of defending the comments, situations, or myself. And it certainly wasn't the time or place. I bit my tongue and understood they were struggling as well. But it had me pull back further within myself. It was getting harder every day, and this just compounded the pressure on me to try and fight.

03.02.19

Hey, Bub, my loving hub.
Day 17, I'm starting to get scared
No matter how hard I try to show I cared.
You're slipping away day by day,
And no matter what, I can't make you stay.
It's so hard to watch you go.
But I love you with all my heart and need you to know
Our life together has been such a gift
And very rare if we had a rift.
A gorgeous home and three amazing kids,
I still reflect on your amazing gifts.
You've been a friend, a lover, and my life.
I just hope you know I'm a very proud wife.
No matter how hard I try to make you stay,
In the end, it's your choice on your final day.
Thank you for all you are, have, did, and gave.
I will take your love to my dying grave.
So rest up, baby, and do what you must.
In the universe and our love I need to trust.
I will do my best to laugh out loud
And my utmost to make you proud.

Eighteen days in, and the director of the unit (Dr 2) advised me of a family meeting the following day to draw the line in the sand and that enough was enough. He told me to have the family write down any questions they felt they needed answered in this meeting, no matter how trivial we felt they may be. This was D-Day!

At 9:30 on Tuesday, February 5, I took a big breath and walked into the meeting room with my notepad and questions. Throughout the whole journey, I had full transparency and encouraged Conrad's family and close friends to attend any meetings and to ask any questions to the doctors for their own peace of mind.

During this meeting, Dr 2 was very direct. His bedside manner was a lot more subdued than other doctors, and for that I was grateful. He laid it all on the table, including discussions of organ donation. He asked, "You seem to be a very open family, and it's not something we generally discuss, but had you thought and discussed Conrad's wishes on this topic?" I had to ask, "If Conrad's organs are shutting down and had so much damage, how could this be a viable option based on your previous advise to us?"

During the meeting, it was said, "Conrad would not want this, or to be a burden to the family and not have a quality of life." And yes, they were correct. Conrad wouldn't want that *if* this was to be his final progressive state. But I still felt strongly that he would progress. I often commented I felt he would get back 90 to 95 per cent of his original ability. Big call so early on, I know.

I sat quietly in this meeting for the most part, allowing others to express anything they felt needed. I was so proud of our daughter when she stepped up to reply to the doctor's question, "What would your father say if his children had to wipe his backside." Her filters really let her down that day. Her quick

53

response was, "He would say, 'You're not wiping my fxxking ass and seeing my big cxxk." I'm not sure whose jaw was the lowest—hers, her grandmother's or mine. But after I laughed, and she let out a big sigh of relief. The doctor said, "There is his legacy," pointing at Chantelle.

The mood was lightened. But when the doctor looked at me and my notepad and said, "I suppose you have a million questions," we were back to the moment. I started off advising that I felt the bedside manner of some of the medical doctors needed to be addressed. When he requested clarification I told him the phrases such as, "brain-dead vegetable," "the coroner signing off certificates," and, "decomposing bodies" were not ones that should be used in situations like this. I did not want it recorded, but I felt it needed to be said. People adamantly disagreed with me as they had not heard these conversations in their visits to the hospital, but my daughter backed me on this wholeheartedly. She was present each time these words were used, and on more than one occasion.

And yes, I had questions.

- You say my husband is brain-dead and a vegetable, but your CT scan and MRI are both inconclusive. Why?
- Your EEG report come back with "scattered" signals. What does that mean?
- You say he had no oxygen to the brain for forty-five minutes, but your reports note a "hypoxic brain injury." If there's no oxygen, wouldn't that be anoxic, not hypoxic?
- You say this is the extent of his recovery. To me, the reports don't back that. Is this based on assumptions? I respect your profession, but is this based on previous patients? Because if so, don't ever assume as every person is different.

had to voice my questions and concerns, but I knew I was almost at the end of the hospital process. I could not continue to go up against the system without having the same proof I was requesting the hospital to show me they didn't have. They didn't have the logic as much as I couldn't show them the emotion. I agreed that if Conrad was to have another cardiac arrest not to resuscitate, but they were to maintain a level of care that was to be no less than it currently was. He was to finish the current course of antibiotics, and we were to see what nature had in store for him. (I silently prayed he had the strength to fight.) It was agreed to, and the course of antibiotics was to finish the following day. This was a very hard day for all of us. I went to bed that night praying Conrad was going to be all right and had the strength in him to fight.

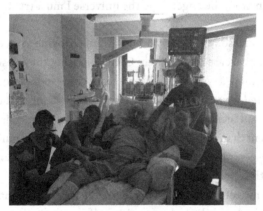

What We Thought Would Be Our Last
Family Photo, February 5 2019

05.02.19

Hey, Bub, day 19, and you're nearing the end.
I dread when I think what's around the next bend.
I'm hurting so much, and it pains me to see.

I wish you had just listened; you'd still be here with me.
We tried so hard to give you the tools,
But I sit and wonder, *Who's the bigger fool?*
Your stubborn attitude will take you to your grave.
It wasn't enough, no matter how much I gave.
You often said I defied you at all cost,
But babe, I never gave up cos our love was not lost.
I don't generally carry anger as an emotion,
But I tell you now, it's running through the motion.
I'm sad, I'm lonely and being torn apart
Cos every day I lose you more, and it's breaking my heart.
I love you more than I could ever say,
So in a poem, I write it every day.
Rest up, baby, and do what you must.
In God, the angels, and the universe I must trust.

On Thursday, February 6, Dr 2 arranged for me to meet with the palliative care team to help Conrad in what they described as his last few days. The palliative team came to his room, but I requested we have the meeting elsewhere. During that day, to me, Conrad seemed to be gurgling and making more noises and movement than previous days. I mentioned this to the nurse and said, "It seems like he is trying to find his voice." I gave Conrad a kiss on the cheek and said, "I will be back shortly, Bub."

On my return an hour later, I could not believe what I saw. Conrad had somehow dragged himself across the bed, and it looked like he was trying to get out of it. It wasn't unusual for him to move involuntarily and be very restless, but today he seemed to be intent on trying to get out of the bed. When I asked the nurse what was the matter and how long he had been like this, her reply was, "As soon as you left the room, he became very distressed." I leaned over to him to provide him comfort and reassurance that I was there. He grabbed my hands, and I heard him say in a very gargled voice and through his tracheotomy, "I w-anna g-ooo h-h-oo-mmm-ee." It was the faintest gargle, but I heard it: "I wanna go home!

I called for the senior doctor immediately. When he entered the room, I told him what had transpired. He did not believe me. He told me it could not have happened and was not what I heard. I looked pleadingly at the nurse, but to no avail. I told the doctor I rescinded our conversation on the Tuesday prior and wanted to fight for him. I had to give him an opportunity to prove he was there. The doctor looked at me and asked if I was 100 per cent sure I wanted to prolong the inevitable. I told him, "My husband is trying to find his voice, and I need to give him time to prove this." The doctor reluctantly agreed. I had it noted and made him repeat my request back to me: "If Conrad goes into cardiac arrest, they are to resuscitate, and if he were to again get an infection, it was to be treated." The nurse on duty stood at his point and confirmed that Conrad had been trying to find his voice throughout the day. I almost burst into tears. I knew how hard that was for her.

Two days later, when Dr 2 passed me in the ICU hallway, he looked at me, pointed, and said, "You are one strong amazing woman. You have never given up."

I looked at him, smiled, and replied, "Dr 2, I will *never* give up!" He gave me a huge hug and went about his rounds.

Recovery after a Storm with the Help of an Angel

I arrived at the hospital early on Monday, February 11 to spend extra time with my husband to be met by a gorgeous new doctor. Doctor 3 had the aura of an angel, and I immediately fell in love with her bubbly persona—and her shoes! She was very much like a hippy, and when she greeted me, she was full of warmth and excitement. She requested I meet with her to go over some things she had concerns about. We went to a meeting room, where she told me how every week prior to her new roster, she obtained patient files to assess the day before her shift was to start. When she read through Conrad's file, she noted how sorry she felt for his family and was dreading the conversation that needed to be had again about letting him go. But to her absolute amazement, she walked into Conrad's room, introduced herself, and was blown away when he said a muffled, "Good morning." This took her very much by surprise as the reports she read did not reflect her morning greeting. This confused her, and she investigated further as to how this could be. She got my input on what I felt his behaviours had been and the timeline of his infections. The course of antibiotics he had been on finished the Wednesday prior, and a day later, I heard him tell me, "I wanna go home." This bought more excitement from her.

In her words, "The universe had aligned." She realised she had, over time, three patients who had the same symptoms of involuntary body movements, thrashing, and nonresponsive behaviours. She did a little research as to what the common link may have been and realised they were all on the same antibiotic, which she described as a fourth-generation antibiotic used only in the ICU. She said it could take up to a week to have the drug out of his system and asked if I noticed improvements each day in his speech and thrashing, which I had. She advised she was going to write a submission to both the medical board of the hospital and the pharmaceutical board to have the drug assessed. We discussed the effects of this drug and previous consequences of others for a while. With her final comment of, "I do not want to go there," she got up, gave me a big hug, and did a happy dance. She left the room to continue on her "gorgeous fairy way."

Two days later, Dr 1 was back on duty. When I asked where Dr 3 was, he advised she was unwell and he was now on roster. I told him what had transpired with Dr 3 and her findings and that the drug used instigated the behaviours in Conrad. Dr 1 told me he would use whatever drug he felt was needed to ensure a patient was receiving the best care. This immediately rang alarm bells with me, and I instructed him *not* to use that drug on my husband. Again he said he would do the best he felt for his patient. I turned to the ICU nurse and requested she check Conrad's file to ensure Dr 3 had made note of an allergy to previous medication. The nurse was hesitant and looked at the doctor for approval. I pushed the point and again requested she check his file. After a nod from Dr 1, she confirmed a note had been put on his file to not use this drug. Phew! I was very relieved.

As each day passed, Conrad became more and more vocal and coherent—and very erratic with his movements. The poor ward staff were called almost hourly to have him either moved back up his bed or to clean him up. He did not sit still. He constantly thrashed or threw his arms and legs around and slid across or down his bed. Doctors said this was all to do with his brain injury and was his limit of progress. He was still very nonresponsive and unable to obey basic commands, but to me, he was progressing daily. He was getting stronger, and his erratic movements were lessening. I felt he settled if I redirected his attention by talking to or calming him. Every time Dr 1 or Dr 2 walked in to do an assessment, I greeted them with the same, "You're surprised, Doctor, aren't you? I'm not going away, Doctor." It became a cheeky ritual for me, but I think it would have given them nightmares.

Another trip to the Gold Coast had Dr Alt work on his brain-to-body communication and energy fields, again by tuning in to his body through me and muscle testing. I mentioned the infections and how often he battled them to be told they were predominately coming in through the catheter and into his bladder. Nothing could be done to remove these outside the hospital. Dr Alt enlisted another naturopath at the health clinic to start to work on Conrad energetically with bio-resonance. I sent a sample of his hair for them to match his DNA to the electromagnetic waves needed to help him. It was mainly focused around infection.

At no point did I discuss what I was doing externally with the doctors at the hospital. I had been advised they could have had me isolated for up to three days if they thought I was interfering with their processes, and all they needed to implement this was a signature from a justice of the peace. My mouth was sealed shut!

February 14, 2019—Valentine's Day

I arrived at the ICU with a whole window of notes written by the nurse caring for Conrad wishing me a Happy Valentine's Day.

My husband had made it four weeks, and this was the best gift ever. I ducked out for a bit around lunchtime, until I received a call at about 1:30 from the ICU staff to advise Conrad was being moved down to the acute ward. This was progress, but very scary as he still needed intensive care. I was advised the care would not be reduced. He would still have a nursing specialist for his own safety and be in a room of his own.

When I arrived back at the hospital and walked into the lift, Conrad was being taken down to the acute ward with two nurses and two ward staff around him to ensure all his monitors were still in place and he was safe. As the bed was wheeled into the ward, I asked the ICU nurse if he was to be assisted by an AIN (assistant in nursing). She gave a definite yes and mentioned he would have a room of his own. As the changeover nurse took control of the bed, he was guided into a room of four. I turned to the ICU nurse, and she quickly handed over his files and was leaving as I started to ask about an AIN. The new nursing staff said they were not aware of such a request, and he would be safe in a room of four with one nurse at the door to monitor him and the three other patients. Conrad had been heavily sedated for his transfer to the acute ward, and at this stage, was asleep and not moving. But would that change over the next hour.

No AIN had been sent, and when I asked the nurses to advise on this, I was dismissed. I requested a doctor to assess Conrad as he was becoming very unsettled the more he woke up. The constant noises and yelling from other patients would have been a challenge for Conrad as he had come from an ICU room of his own and with complete silence. Every movement was heightened, and he almost fell out of the bed because of the small side rails. The other three patients in the room were also very vocal and had their own challenges. I watched in horror for the next hour as the poor nurse ran from patient to patient. I sat there in absolute shock. The nurse looked at me and said, "Welcome to the room from hell."

A doctor came to assess him around 5 p.m., after my repeated requests. When she saw him constantly moving, she asked, "What is he doing?" Ummm, hello. "This is him at his best. He will get worse with involuntary movements, and it is not safe for him to be unattended." The doctor said she was not aware of this, and she was not happy as he had been sedated and felt those in the new ward were misinformed about his needs. And she would not commit to an AIN as the paperwork did not show need for it. Then she left for the day. WTF?

Our daughter arrived about 5:30, and the look on my face must have said it all. I gave her a run through on the afternoon events, and she said, "Leave it with me. I'm going upstairs to the ICU to sort this." Within fifteen minutes, she was back and said, "Sorted!" Apparently she had gone to ICU and had a conversation with the social worker and doctor. She had them see reason to support an AIN to ensure Conrad's ongoing safety. She has some mongrel in her when she gets on her soapbox. One very proud mum and so grateful she took over on this one.

Over the next hour, and as Conrad regained consciousness, the vocals kicked in. He was getting stimulated by all the background noise, and every time the nurse reprimanded Thomas (another patient) for pulling his tubes out, Conrad would laugh and also yell at Thomas. Conrad still had no vision, and his speech was very incoherent. And to hear him trying to get involved in his surroundings was humorous, at the time. This was when I really noticed Conrad's personality starting to come back with a cheekier side. He managed to understand the conversations around him and put his input into them. Our daughter commented on Conrad's behaviour, and he was quick to tell her, "Back it up, angel girl!" Though it was very muffled, it was understandable. Throughout this journey, I took photos and notes daily. One of my favourite three photos was taken on that day as I asked him for a kiss and to "Pucker up, baby."

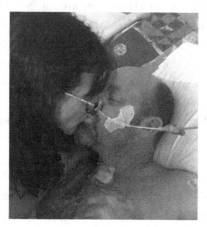

Pucker Up, Baby! Valentine's Day 2019

When he wasn't focused on a topic or listening to our conversation, Conrad was trying to get out of the bed and pull his tubes out. We constantly had to engage him by talking to him. It was exhausting getting up every minute and pushing him back into his bed as he tried to get over the sides. I left the hospital at eight that evening with our daughter, and only after he was moved to a room of his own with a specialist nurse to ensure he did not get out of bed.

Conrad had developed very bad muscle spasms the more he progressed. The spasms were so strong and had him throwing his head from side to side constantly. He could not sleep, and if he did, it was in very short bursts. I told the kids that on my next trip to the Gold Coast, I would see if the doctor could assist with these spasms to help him sleep, if nothing else. Dr Alt worked on his brain-to-body communication and said that his muscles were "conflicting." He had a dominant muscle that was the reactor, bullying the other muscles in that group, causing them to loop. He had ten different muscle patterns, and each pattern had up to ten muscles in that group to cause the spasm. She ascertained that one main muscle in each group was stopping the others from working, but individually, they worked. I felt like the doctor was driving a car as she used my arms to act as each of Conrad's muscles in the group and reactivated them to work independently. As with each appointment, I was given an approximate time for each session to integrate into Conrad's energy body. This was to take up to seven days, but she noted we should see improvement within two to three days.

Conrad progressed daily in all areas. But as he did, other areas became more of a concern. He constantly tried to get out of the bed. And as he had no strength or muscle tone, this was a safety issue. He was becoming more aware of the tubes in his body and constantly tried to pull them out. This caused infections and internal bleeding in his urinary tract. Hallucinations had come on, so he was constantly awake and in a state of distress.

Within a few days, the spasms had definitely lessened, so much so that the kids commented that the two main muscles on either side of the neck had almost stopped their constant movements. This gave him some relief, and he slept a little. Thank you, Dr Alt.

I returned to work after about four to six weeks to try and find some balance at home and to catch up on my role as financial controller for a labour hire company. I worked from 7:30 to 11:30/12.00. Then I drove to the hospital each afternoon, where I stayed with him until 7 or 8 p.m. each day.

It was interesting on any day to go in and be part of his journey at that time. Sometimes he he was back in his retail days, pending a visit from head office management. And if I didn't adhere to his commands of moving the clothing racks, he would get quite frustrated. Another time we were heading off camping, and when he couldn't put the fuel pump into the car or the car keys wouldn't fit in the ignition, he was again very cranky. The whole time, the family and nurses had to try and play along with any journey he embarked on that day. One day I turned up and apparently interrupted a very important meeting. After I asked, "Hey honey, how are you today?" he responded, "Shut up! I'm in a meeting. Right, who is doing the sales marketing? We need to subdivide and sell these blocks." He went on for a good half hour. I sat and only inputted when asked. When our son Liam called to say hi and I told him Dad was in a meeting and apparently today he is a property developer, I got "the look" and a very stern, "Fxxing smart Ass." Then he went back to his meeting. The journey we took on any day was very imaginative, but in his mind, they were very real. We always had a laugh.

Dr 1 from the ICU, popped in a few days after Conrad was moved to the acute ward, and I just couldn't help myself. "You're surprised, aren't you Dr 1? I'm not going away, Dr 1. Have they moved you out of ICU now, Dr 1?" Dr 1 told me he popped in to check on his "friend" and his progress.

After a week in a room of his own, they moved him into a room of four as the rehabilitation team could not take him until he proved he was okay to be monitored by a nurse with three other patients. On day 1, his first attempt failed, along with the second and third. He constantly tried to get out of the bed. And he did not know where he was. Nor was he retaining information when we did tell him. He was also hallucinating quite badly. On the fourth attempt, we had progress, but he found his tubes to be more annoying. I got a text midmorning from another patient's family, whom I had befriended in the ICU: "Your husband is fxxing hilarious. He has just lost his shxt with the nurses and called them all fxxxwits." Oh no!

I arrived at around 1 p.m. to a nurse requesting my assistance in putting his nasal gastric tube back in. He had pulled it out during the night, and all attempts to reinsert it earlier that day had failed. Hmm. Conrad was tube fed, so this meant he hadn't eaten all day. This was a concern. The nurses often commented that I had the ability to settle him, so they thought it best to leave it until I could assist. This is where the humour really starts to come in as I realised my husband no longer had "filters" with what he was saying and to whom. His speech was still very slurred, but I could just make out what he was trying to say. Sometimes we had to get him to repeat it. His best friend, Tony, came for his regular visit and stepped off to the left foot of the bed so that the nurse and I could put the tube in. As Conrad started gagging and dry retching, Tony did the same, while laughing. Conrad still had no vision or understanding as to what was going on. All he heard was laughter and me trying not to laugh while assuring him about what was going on. The nurse was to the right, and Conrad started pointing fiercely at him, asking, "Whose idea was this fxxing party trick?" This bought on more laughter. And as all Conrad heard was Tony's voice, he assumed it was Tony doing the deed. The next statements out of Conrad's mouth were, "You're fxxing dead, Tony. If this is your idea, I'm gunna punch you in the fxxing face," all while he was gagging and dry retching. After the tube was back in place, we all saw the funny side—once we explained it to Conrad again.

We got through that one, but during the night, he again pulled out the tube. And with the lack of nutrients, this clogged up the back end. So a tube went in the top end along with a suppository in the back end. We laughed at the nasal tube yesterday, and this was even funnier. I stood outside the screen while the wardsmen and nurses did their duty in putting the suppository in, not an easy task. I had been told during this journey that the back end is the first to go under such trauma and is one of the last to come back online in regards to the mind knowing when it needs to work. So when Conrad told me about thirty minutes later he needed to shxt, I got very excited. My reply was, "Babe, that's awesome. You actually know you need to go to the toilet. I am so excited." His reply was, "No, I *need* to go to the toilet. You don't understand, I *need* to go to the toilet." I grabbed the nurse to tell her, and she called for the wardsmen again.

His need to go was quicker than the call for the wardsmen. I reassured him that he had sanitary pants on that allowed for this, but he knew that it was not something he used to do. He was getting a little distressed trying to tell me how much he needed to go. Finally I said, "Just go in your pants, and the nurse will clean it up when you are done." The next five minutes there was silence and a few movements. When he asked, "So now what?" I smiled and said, "We wait for the staff." This got a look of horror from Conrad and a response of, "So I have to sit in it?" As he took in a big breath of air, he choked out, "And it stinks!" It took a while for him to be cleaned up. The laughter was shared by all in the room of four as Conrad was very vocal during the whole ordeal. Even Conrad found the funny side—once he was comfortable again.

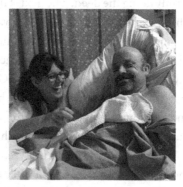

No matter what, we always found humour!

Every day we had laughter, no matter what the situation. We have always found the funny side of most situations. And as Conrad got better, we found more situations most people would not find so funny. That was what got us through the eating disorder with our daughter, and this was no different. It certainly wasn't the response the nurses expected. Our family humour was admired by his carers. They understood this was our way of dealing with the situation and how we interacted as a family. I had also made a booklet for any of Conrad's carers to write in, and it also told them who he was. It received great feedback as it allowed the nurses to have a conversation with him and redirect him to what was fact. If he felt he was a retail manager and at work, they could tell him he worked for Transport and Main Roads as a business manager. They also had the ability to make notes on Conrad's day if they felt the need.

One night a new patient was put in the room of four. Based on what nurses said, she had a history or being very difficult. Throughout the night she screamed and was very unsettled. As Conrad had recently come from the ICU and a very quiet room, he did not take this very well. I received a call from his physiotherapist at 8:30 the next morning, advising Conrad wouldn't settle and to see if I could assist over the phone. He settled enough to work for the therapist during the session, but when I arrived at the hospital around two that afternoon, I was horrified. Conrad was lying across the bed with several nurses and doctors over him in distress. It broke my heart to see him in this state, and I immediately went to reassure and settle him. He had managed to break the bed in trying to get out, and the medical staff didn't know how to settle him or why he was so distressed. I took his hand and requested all the staff to step away and give him some room as he did not like people in his personal space. I talked to him and reassured he was safe and overtired. It only took me a couple of minutes to calm him enough to have him transitioned to another bed. The social worker had been contacted by the doctor during this, and they realised it was the overstimulation caused by a sleepless night and the other patient screaming. They arranged to have him moved to an single room again.

Within the hour, Conrad was relocated to the rehabilitation and stroke ward of the hospital. He had an AIN and a room of his own. He settled well. Over the next week, Conrad became more alert, but his vision and memory were still concerns. Each week I travelled the three hours round trip to go to the Gold Coast to see my "guru," as Conrad always called my alternate therapists. She was blown away at how fast Conrad was progressing. We never had expectations but were always pleased at his daily progress. Nothing ever surprised me when he achieved the "unachievable."

Doctors were very baffled as to his progress. They could not explain how he had recovered to this extent and had no idea of how far he would recover. Every day I got the, "This is where he is, and this is what you have got!"

One week in the stroke unit saw small progress, but as Conrad had a brain injury and this was a stroke rehab, they did not have the full ability to help him. He was on the waitlist to be moved to a rehabilitation unit (RU) at another hospital, but they could not take him until he was off a specialist nurse, so this was a catch-22. Conrad could not be left alone as he constantly moved, tried to get out of the bed, and had no vision or understanding of consequences.

The social worker, Miss SW1 (Social Worker 1), was amazing, and I related well to her. After some personal discussions, we found we had a lot in common. She was a force and took on our plight to have Conrad moved to the RU as soon as possible. Every week all the rehab centres have a conference call to discuss incoming patients and their directions about discharging current patients. As a specialist facility that caters to patients from several states, and with a fantastic reputation in what they do, I was told this could take months.

March 4 was my weekly trip to the Gold Coast. I enjoyed the three-hour round drive. I could switch off and just listen to music. I was always keen to see what the next priority was for Conrad in his journey, and for the doctor to ensure I was managing okay energetically. This week Dr Alt worked on his vision to try and help him see a bit better. And she again worked on brain-to-body communication and body-to-brain communication. As Conrad's surrogate, the doctor had me hold up a book and lift my leg while trying to read. I was unable to do more than one of these at the same time. After some clearing of blockages and working energetically, I was able to hold my leg up, hold the book, and read what was on the page. She advised it would take up to seven days to integrate into his body, and within that time, Conrad should be able to do a "three-step command." Previously, he could do a one-step command, 1 task at a time.

On March 6, I got a call at work at 9 a.m. to say they were moving him to the new hospital by 11 a.m. I was over the moon. I arrived at the stroke unit in time to help him eat a yogurt and see the paramedics transfer him to the ambulance. Miss SW did an amazing job in consultation with Miss SW2 at the rehab unit. And much to my surprise, he had a room of his own and ongoing support in an AIN. I was excited to have him in the best facility and to give him the tools to progress.

First coffee in a new hospital.

I arrived at the new hospital after Conrad was taken by ambulance, and to say I was overwhelmed is an understatement. This hospital is massive.

On first impression, the nurses were lovely. I felt comfortable in where Conrad was—even though the hospital was intimidating for me—and excited about the next chapter in his journey. What made it a little easier was that three weeks prior to Conrad being moved there, a good friend's father had also been admitted to the same hospital, but on the other side in a different unit. Billy become a regular visitor for Conrad and a coffee date for me.

On the second day of Conrad being at rehab unit, the doctors at the facility assessed him for their own records. I sat and watched and listened as the doctor relayed details to his assistant for inputting into the computer. I was very impressed when one of the assessments came up with, "A three-step command." Woohoo! I had never heard this terminology until earlier that week, and Dr Alt said Conrad would progress to it. In the assessment, Conrad showed the doctor he could lift his leg and arm at the same time while doing a third task. This was huge for me and validation that going to the Gold Coast each week was worth it. Every day he progressed, and I was bursting with pride and learning so much myself.

I decided that as this was to be my next new home away from home, I would bring my guitar to entertain Conrad when he got bored and to take my mind off things. I also put affirmations on the wall at the end of his bed for nurses to read to him and for him to read as his vision had started to come on intermittently. I thought it may help him understand where he was. The notes had things such as: "I have had a cardiac arrest," "I am in hospital," "I am a finance and operations manager for TMR." I felt the ten things I selected were bullet points to help redirect him when he was hallucinating and delusional.

After dinner and a shower one night, I sat playing guitar for Conrad when the biggest grin broke out on his face as he looked around the room. I looked around, trying to figure out what he was seeing. After a few minutes, and with the grin getting bigger, he started to point his finger and count. I asked what he was seeing. He replied in a very low whisper, "There are seven of them, all in wheelchairs, and they are here listening to me play the guitar." There was no one in the room, but in his mind's eye, they certainly were. At the end of each song, he smiled as he looked around the room and clapped. Apparently the audience did too. He looked so very proud at that moment. It was very sweet.

His hallucinations were bad. Doctors were baffled as to why he was having them. They started asking questions about the medication he was taking. I told them, "I have no idea the doctors at the previous hospital put him on that." It turned out Conrad was on an opiate patch, and the doctor was confused as it is a pain suppressant. He asked if Conrad experienced a lot of pain. It had me thinking about the night before he was transferred to RU. He had a really bad night with hallucinations, and I received a phone call from the nurses in the very early hours of the morning to try and settle him as the medication did not relax or sedate him enough to sleep. He had only had the new patch put on that day. It made me ask the new doctor if the medication could be causing the hallucinations. He replied with a, "Not usually. But if he was coming off it, there was more of a chance." He said the medication was to supress any pain and until he was off it, we wouldn't know if Conrad was, in fact, in pain.

Dr 4 had the patch taken off, and the very next morning, Conrad complained of chest pains. Here we go again! Panic stations hit, and he was sent off for X-rays, blood tests, and ultrasounds to see if he had another heart attack. All came back clear, but within two days, the same thing occurred. I told the doctor I had been saying for years that I felt Conrad had suffered from angina as he often had chest pains. Each time he went to the doctor, he was told he didn't have angina. The pains did settle over the next week or so, and when he did have an attack, he was given nitrate to help open up the airways. Dr 4 suggested that maybe he had been misdiagnosed up to this point and that he felt Conrad did fact suffer from angina. The nitrate seemed to help when he had an attack, but it didn't help settle my nerves any though.

As I sat one afternoon watching Conrad sleep, I opened the Facebook page that I had created the week or so before Conrad went down. He motivated me do this and my webpage and he challenged me to finish a task. I was bought to tears when I noted a recommendation put on the page January 16, the day before he went down. Conrad had recommended "Tereasa has an amazing ability to get yourself to challenge your own emotions and behaviours. You will find all your answers within. I had not seen this as it was one of the first times I actually opened the page, and it was eight weeks later. It bought a tear to my eye as I remembered the two weeks at the start of this year, prior to his arrest, and where we were as a couple along with our personal growth. I smiled, but I was also sad.

After about a week at the new unit, and as I sat playing the guitar, I noticed Conrad get very anxious. He started to rub his head and tried to shrink in his environment. He curled up, and it looked like he was cowering in his bed. I requested the nurse take his observations. His blood pressure had increased, and he was all clammy. As I watched him, I wondered if the increasing storm activity outside was causing this. When the first clap of lightning hit, I knew that was the cause. Prior to Conrad's arrest, he would be the first to sit in the middle of the backyard and watch a storm roll in. Today it had him almost out of his skin. He was terrified. I took him out to the dining area in his wheelchair to take him out of the isolated room. When we got there, he kept trying to look around. Not being able to see, he asked me if he was near any walls or windows. The storm passed about an hour later, and as it did, he settled more.

The following day I did my usual weekly trip to the Gold Coast, and again it was found Conrad was in fight or flight and had left his body. The storm had caused him to panic. He was put back in energetically, and Dr Alt worked on more of his brain and brain-to-body communication. The muscle spasms had drastically reduced to the point where they didn't seem to be an issue for him, so other priorities became foremost. Dr Alt tuned in to Conrad energetically and worked on what was resonating with her at that time. She also continued to check in on me and make sure I was doing okay.

I got daily phone calls from family suggesting I could not continue to be at the hospital every day and constant expressions of their concerns for my health and safety. I acknowledged their concerns, but I always trusted myself and in my ability to push forward. I actually enjoyed the challenge, and it was well worth it to walk into the hospital daily and see my husband smiling back at me. The nurses and therapists often commented on how much of a difference my being there made to their sessions and to Conrad's continued progress.

On the way back from the Gold Coast, I saw a storm brewing over the city. It was 1 p.m. I called the unit to tell them to keep an eye on Conrad as I had noticed behavioural changes when there were storms around. The nurses acknowledged it with a little hesitation in their voices. Within a half hour, I received a phone call from them asking me to settle him as he was very distressed, and they couldn't understand what triggered this change so quickly. When I told them again about the storm activity, they listened. I was only ten minutes from his room, and knowing I was on my way was enough to settle him. I arrived at his bed, and he was very panicked. He wouldn't let me go. I kept reassuring him this was due to the storm activity. I asked for the doctor to pop in when he was available.

The doctor came to his room not long after, and when I asked if the storm activity could be causing his already sensitive brain to react, Dr 5 said, "Studies had actually proven that the earth's magnetic energy can have an effect on a brain, and more so in such a sensitive state. The full moon also has patients act very different from any other day." He had no doubt the storm could be having an impact on Conrad's brain and sensitivities. Later that night, when I returned home, I did some research on essential oils to help with the brain and overstimulation and made a blend to take in the next day.

I was grateful that Dr 5 listened to my crazy thoughts about the brain. When I told him I made the blend and wanted his approval to use it, he was happy with the mix but advised against using a few other oils due to their blood-thinning properties and their roles in reducing blood pressure. It was great to be heard and get his approval. The oil was used anytime Conrad showed overstimulation. The feedback from the nurses was very positive.

The hallucinations didn't go; they seemed to be occur often, and he would get very distressed. I would get phone calls at all hours of the night when he was in a state of panic. He felt he was in a burning service station, and I needed to come and save him. Or he was trying to save kids from drowning in the floods at the local Coles car park. Another time he was sitting on a bench and getting upset at all the people laughing at him. He kept telling me he wasn't drunk, and I needed to believe him and to come and get him. In thirty years, I had only seen him intoxicated once, and to hear the tone of his voice and how upset he was in trying to defend himself as not being drunk made me feel for him. He was distressed daily. The doctors tried to adjust his medication to alleviate the hallucinations and the bad dreams he woke up with nightly. The nurses tried not to call me during the night and did their best to settle him. But on several occasions, I got calls throughout the night, sometimes five or six times. They would manage to get an hour sleep out of him and then go through the whole process again. The nurses couldn't apologise enough for waking me, but they had no other way of settling him. They used to smile and say I was better than Risperidone when it came to helping him sleep.

On several occasions, as many as five nurses were trying to settle him and keep him safe in his bed. He would be directing them to pack the car for camping, move racks around the retail store for the big bosses' visit, or help in the boat with all the crocodiles around. They went on many such adventures. Camping and fishing were the most dominant of his dreams and often the most distressing for him as there were crocodiles around. On other occasions, there were fires and burning buildings around him or car accidents. During the day, however,

TEREASA CHATHAM

he seemed more settled, and according to the nurses, more so when I was there.

Conrad progressed, and it showed daily in his continued strength and determination. His therapists were fantastic with him, and I made a point of attending his therapies daily. His physiotherapy session was often scheduled mid-afternoon to help me attend. Miss Phys was great with him, and on day 1, I told all the therapists they were not to take it easy on him. He would only progress if given a challenge, and they were to "ride his backside" if he slackened off. This worked. Conrad was still very competitive and each week we set goals for him. On several occasions, he had these blitzed by the Tuesday of that week. The doctors still did not know how far he would recover as he was already past anything they could dream he would get to. I smiled daily as I knew he would continue to impress.

Daily therapy sessions.

Each day I arrived at the unit to attend his therapy, entertain him for the afternoon, and take him out to have his dinner at 5 p.m. After tea, I took him in for what affectionately became his "personal pamper pack" with toileting, a shower, shave, deodorising, dressing, foot massage with body butter, a head massage with oil blends, and a lavender dab on his shirt. We finished off with a nice chamomile tea, medication (by nurse), and bed by 7 or 7:30. Then I left to drive the hour home.

I looked forward to Conrad's assessment each day and how he explained his day to me. One day on arriving I noticed he had a shave and a haircut. Not only had they shaved his face, it seemed they had also run the shaver up and over the top of his head. When I asked him the next day how his day had been, he ran his hand over his head and said, "They took a blowtorch and burnt my hair off." I tried really hard not to laugh as he told me this; he was very serious. I asked him to explain how this happened. According to him, they had taken him out to the local shopping centre, and in a very descriptive and verbal way, he moved his arms around and over his head, making the noises of a blowtorch to describe it. Over the next few days, and with each visitor, he did the same, again to much laughter. When I ran my hand over his head, the stubble could be mistaken for hair growing back after it was burnt.

April 4, 2019, Eleven Weeks In

Progression daily and impressing to no end. Two weeks prior, a new patient arrived in the unit who heard me playing the guitar for Conrad. He smiled as he walked past the room, and I introduced Conrad and myself to him. His name was Kevin, and when I asked if he liked music, he said he used to play guitar. But due to injuries, the doctors told him he would never play again. I offered to let him borrow my guitar and give it a go, but he commented there was no point. The next day I popped in with my guitar and dropped it on his lap. The biggest smile came on his face when his fingers actually plucked at the guitar. That was the start of daily jam sessions. I brought another guitar in from home and left it in the room with Kevin, and he often enjoyed playing during the day. It certainly made his time a lot easier. He often commented how the guitar had, "saved his life." Conrad and Kevin became "meal buddies," and it gave me comfort knowing Conrad had someone to chat with.

Kevin often filled me in on the night-time activities that went on in Conrad's room. We often laughed at how often Conrad would yell, "I need a piss." Conrad was still on a hoist with to transfer from bed to chair, and as it was easier than calling the wardsmen every hour for a toilet break, a bottle was used. We had several interesting situations with the bottle. I learned quickly to explain to Conrad every intention and movement that I was going to do. On one occasion, I had placed the bottle for Conrad to go to the toilet but forgot to tell him I was taking it away after he finished. When I pulled it away, he lost his mind and starting yelling at me, telling me how stupid I was and why would I now pour it all over him? The bottle was in my hand, still full, but in his mind, it was otherwise. He would pat his stomach and groin and try to grab my hand to feel, saying, "Feel it. It's wet. You think it's funny to pour it all over me?" I couldn't help but laugh. But boy did he go off and did I get in trouble. I never forgot to tell him what each of my movements were after that.

Another time the male nurse took too long in asking our boys to leave the room, put on his gloves, and find the bottle. All the while, Conrad was holding himself, saying, "Hurry up. I need a piss." The boys could hear him from outside the room as the nurse gave the okay to urinate. Unfortunately, the nurse put the bottle on upside down, and as soon as it went into the bottle, it flowed straight back out of the bottle. And there was another rant of, "You think this is funny? Are you a fxxing idiot?

Why would you do that?" The boys were beside themselves with laughter. When we told Conrad about his antics on returning to the room, he laughed and didn't remember it all.

When other patients grabbed me on my way into his room and express their sleepless nights and his carrying on, I would ask him how he slept. He would reply, "Fine. I had a great night's sleep." "Hmm," I used to say. "Opinions varied," and explained otherwise. We always found humour. Always! Not everyone understood this, but this was how our family dealt with life—good and bad.

Conrad's best friend, Tony, popped in weekly, along with other good friends Andrew and Mark. Mark's dad, Billy, tried to come by every couple of days to see him when I was there. I was often shocked at where the conversations would go. With a brain injury, there are no filters, and the poor nurses would have to endure talk from how big his bowel movements were on the day to who was wiping his backside. I would often give the nurse the heads-up as a conversation started and I had no idea as to where it would go. But we always laughed.

After he just finished telling the nurse and myself one afternoon that his, "ass was itchy. Some idiot gave me a new asshole the night before when they wiped me." I smiled and told him that it was me. He went, "Oops," as he tried to rub his butt on the bed to alleviate the itch. I offered for the nurse to get some cream and I would rub it on him to sooth the itch. As I turned around to finish the request with the nurse, I heard behind me, "I'm ready!" I turned around to see him on all fours, his pants down, and his backside pointing to the corridor. At that stage, he couldn't sit or roll, so I have no idea how he found the strength to roll over and get on all fours. I almost fell over laughing, as did the nurse. Conrad has always been a very private and conservative person, so for him to be so open and vocal about personal topics was a very light side to him and always brought laughter. No matter who was present.

His vision was intermittent, so we had trouble when he was hallucinating. For weeks, anytime he woke at night or during the day, he yelled at the nurses and me to clean his bed of all the sand and to get him off the beach. One night the nurses called me to try settle him as he thought he was at a BP service station that was on fire. He was very distressed.

Each day I watched him intently trying to figure out how and why he had these thoughts and try to understand what his brain was doing. As I sat at his bed one day, looking out his door into the corridor, I noticed the wall directly opposite him was cream in colour. There was a light blue rail. A picture of a beach setting and rocks hung on the wall. A little to the right was a green sign with the room and bed number of the room opposite. I started to think maybe the beach that he felt he was at were actually the images he saw. But his brain, not knowing where he was, put it all together that he was at the beach. The cream wall was the colour of sand, and the blue was very much the colour of water or the sky. The green signage happened to be the same colour green you saw at a BP service station. And again I wondered if this could be Conrad's mind trying to piece everything together without having all the information at hand.

As mentioned, his vision was very intermittent. One day he would tell you what he seen clearly, and on other days, nothing at all. Although it was obvious that his vision was better if he was looking straight ahead rather that to either side. I approached the doctors the next day about my thoughts. One doctor was intrigued and supported my thought process. The other asked if we faced him out the window looking at the garden, would he see a jungle? Maybe we should have tried it!

I learned fairly quickly I needed to find another way to redirect Conrad and for him to try and trust his other senses.

I started to work hard with him when he wasn't clear on his surroundings. I had him close his eyes, feel around with his hand, and to trust the voices around him. After much training, he finally realised that if he closed his eyes and felt to the right, he would feel a wall and then drop lower to feel the bed rail. Reach lower, and he could feel the bed. All under our verbal command. This worked well at night when he would listen to us trying to redirect him, whether it was the nurse or me on the phone. He became used to the feel of his surroundings, and it made it easier. For a short time.

When his vision worked and he could see a little, the quilt I made gave him comfort and familiarity whenever he returned to what he thought was not his room. The quilt was always on his bed, and because it is very bright, it automatically validated that he was in his room every time he saw it. Conrad was happy whenever he had it. I often told him that it was a direct line to me, which gave him comfort. Over the weeks, I often saw him cuddled up to the quilt and sleeping peacefully> The nurses often commented on how it helped him by giving him security.

One day after working and very exhausted, I turned up at the hospital to a very agitated patient. He constantly tried to get out of the bed. I just sat, and he would be trying to get out of bed. Then I would have to stand up and guide him back to his pillow. I also found that having to answer the same question a hundred times gets quite tiring as well. I was *not* in the mood for attitude. And when he asked what time his therapy was for the tenth time in about ninety seconds, I was a little short with him. His appointment was at 2:30, and I told him it was 2:40. He looked at his bare wrist and told me they were running late, and his watch had fallen off his wrist. Feeling around his bed, he found what he thought was the watch—it was invisible to me—and no matter how many times I asked him to close his eyes and feel between his fingers, to him, the watch was real. He grabbed me and pulled me to his face. He told me he was about to throw the fxxxing watch at me and that it was stuck between his fingers. When he showed me a gap between his thumb and pointer finger, I cracked and replied, "Throw it at me. It won't hurt cos it's invisible!" I was called a "smart ass," and he pushed his wrist into my face and asked, "What time is it?" My reply, "Fxxxing invisible o'clock." It about ten minutes later, he threw his hands in the air, with, "You're right. There is no watch." Really?

This one is one of my favourite videos that I recorded over his journey. He laughs each time he watches it, no pun intended. From very early on, I was advised to record his journey and progress in therapy to be able to show him his progress along the way. We got a lot of great photos and videos, and some very unexpected humorous moments.

Andrew popped in weekly to see his progress and join in his physio sessions, and he soon became a target for one session. Conrad had to throw a beanbag into buckets on either side of Andrew by about a meter. To me, it was boring. I told his therapist that unless it was a challenge, Conrad wouldn't put much effort in. So I suggested that she make Conrad have to hit Andrew in the head with each throw. Conrad and Andrew had a very competitive fitness relationship prior to his arrest, so both played the game. Andrew egged him on with comments. The first few throws, Conrad couldn't quite get the direction right as they flew over Andrew's head and shoulders. Then one hit Andrew in the chest and then in the chin and nose. This put a bit of fun into the session. Andrew always loved to challenge Conrad, and it was accepted wholeheartedly.

Miss Phys loved the laughter in each session and brought her own challenges to his sessions. She often asked him to close his eyes as she moved around the room, and when he opened them, he was to throw the beanbag for her to catch. We realised pretty quickly that Conrad had tuned in to her shoes on the floor, and he knew straight away what direction to look. So after a few goes at this, the shoes came off. And then her key tag to lots of laughter. He was getting cheeky. Conrad learned quickly how to work with his vision impairment and trust his ears. On good days, and when he had a decent night's sleep, he had partial vision, but it was very frustrating for him. One of the best sessions we had, his therapist hid bright yellow and orange beanbag balls around the room at body height, while also having blue and pink beams and planks as obstacles on the ground. Without the challenge in it, he hit the obstacles. There was no consequence, so I suggested for her to mark him on his session. I advised that each beanbag could be worth five points and hitting an obstacle took two points off his score. We noticed a very direct and quick change in his movement, sight, and ability. There were seven beanbags and a total of thirty-five points up for grabs. The first day he hit five obstacles, so he scored 25/35. The second day it was 31/35. Watching him on his third day was hilarious. He was tiptoed with the greatest of ease to ensure he didn't hit any obstacles, and he scanned with accuracy to find each beanbag. Miss Phys and I had a great laugh. And credit to him, he scored 35/35.

Toward the end of March, Conrad started to get more movement and was able to roll himself over in the bed. But this brought about a new challenge of dizzy spells on almost every rollover. He did not lie still for five minutes, and every time he went to adjust in the bed and make himself comfortable, I had to stand and assist, and settle him as the head spins almost made him fall out of bed. This was very tiring for both of us, especially when he just would not settle in the evening. Some nights it took up to an hour to finally get him to sleep. And this didn't include the time it took to feed him and shower him. I left most nights between seven and eight absolutely exhausted, and I still had an hour's drive home and dinner to sort for myself.

After a few days of the dizziness getting worse, and it finally happened in his physio session. I had the therapist do a few tests on him. They wanted to see what his reactions were when they rolled him. Immediately, he felt sick and as if he was going to fall off the bed. The head therapist wasn't sure if it was a neurological signal from the brain that was causing this or if crystals in his inner ear were being dislodged possibly due to a fall. It was arranged to have him assessed the following day by another physiotherapist who we affectionately called the "Dizzy Physy" as she specialised in dizzy spells.

During the next appointment, Conrad was placed on a large bed, and from a sitting position, quickly thrown on his back by two physios to see how his eyes adjusted to the quick movement. He was then rolled quickly to one side with their assistance. It turned out the eyes continued to roll in his head, causing the dizziness and nausea he had been experiencing. According to the Dizzy Physy, the quick movements, if her assessment was right, would put the crystals back into place and should reduce the dizziness for him. Over the next week, noticeable improvements happened, and a further three sessions of the treatment were arranged.

When Conrad was having the first session, I was discussing vertigo with the physio and mentioned my mother had been tested in a large machine in a Sydney hospital that spun her around as she was in it. It was a conversation that continued throughout his treatment. On returning to his room, Conrad got a visit from Tony and decided to explain what the Dizzy Physy did to him. He began by saying that he was, "nailed to a really big, round board and spun around like you would see at a pub chook raffle, or the old 'Plukka Duck on Hey Hey it's Saturday!'" I almost fell off my chair as Tony and I erupted in fits of laughter. I have no idea how he came up with that as a session, but I can only assume my discussion with the therapist about my mum having been put into a large machine and spun had somehow lodged in his mind to some extent. As with his hair being burnt by a blowtorch, this also got good airtime when visitors arrived and lots of laughter. Tony was often the recipient and encouraged it with fits of laughter.

The physical side of therapies Conrad loved, but he struggled with the speech and occupational therapy sessions. To him, these were boring and of no use. Credit to him though; he did do them as he understood it was what was needed to get him home sooner, although his frustrations showed often.

Into April I started to question the doctors on where the investigations were regarding his heart. I needed to know how much damage had been done to his heart and our direction going forward. By this stage, the doctors indicated that they were comfortable with my abilities to support him for day passes to spend time with me and the family outside the unit. This was exciting but also nerve-wracking as nothing had been discussed with his heart. When I bought the subject up, I was told, "He is on optimal heart treatment," and as he was a heart patient at H1, I needed to follow up with them. The following day I called H1 to get their direction on him and to see when he was to have a follow-up with the specialist. I was advised he was no longer a patient of H1. The last notes on file were from back in February, so they were unable to assist with my queries.

The doctors at the H2 were advised of my phone call and eventually arranged ultrasounds on the two arteries that run up either side of the neck and to the heart. They came back with the all clear. Yeah!

On April 8, 2019, an EEG was ordered for the brain signals as Conrad had been having muscle spasms in his legs and arms. Doctors were unsure if they were brain activity and a seizure, or if they were just muscle spasms and part of his progress. I took him over in his wheelchair, along with his AIN for assistance, to have the test done. As we sat in the waiting room a nurse came out and was looking around for a patient. As she looked a little confused, I asked her, "Who are you looking for?" When she replied, "Conrad," I pointed to the wheelchair next to me and said, "This is my husband, Conrad." She directed us into her room, all the while shaking her head. She continued to look confused. When we got in and settled, we started chatting as she put the sensors around his skull. I asked her, "How many hypoxic brain-injured patients have you done EEGs on?" She looked at Conrad and me and replied, "A lot, but only ever in the ICU."

After she finished putting all the sensors in place and started the testing, she picked up his file and started to read it with a very confused look on her face. I took great pleasure in explaining our journey and how proud I was of Conrad and his progress to date, and that I felt he would get back to 90 to 95 per cent of his original health status. He had certainly defied any medical logic, and the reports did not reflect what she saw in front of her. I always smiled when I saw the look on anyone's face when they read his reports and then looked at him with a very puzzled expression.

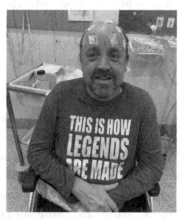

Off for an EEG.

All reports came back with activity in the brain. The spasms in his legs and arms were not seizure-0related, which was comforting to know.

Progress forward again this week with Conrad being able to transition into his beloved Colorado. This is another step towards a day pass out of the hospital. It brought him to tears to see the car that is his pride and joy. He was cheeky enough to ask the physio if he could take it for a drive as he moved along the car toward the driver's seat. Miss Phys was very quick to turn him around and head him in the opposite direction while we all laughed.

Twelve weeks down, and today the doctors took off the AIN for the afternoon shift (2 p.m. to 11 p.m.). I couldn't complain, as up to now, he had an AIN every day, and we were very grateful of that. Conrad struggled with this change and called me six times throughout the night. As usual, I stayed at the hospital until around 8 p.m., so he only had to manage for three hours with the normal hospital nurses and one nurse to four patients. Even such a small change had him very stressed. Over the next few days, he settled more and managed to sleep for the few hours after I left. But the nightmares each night put extra pressure on the nursing team.

Twelve weeks in, and I started to get tired. I'm not sure if it was the one to five nightly phone calls or the fact I worked each morning and then drove to the hospital each day. I had also found lumps in my breast in March, which was not unusual for me, but they added to my pressures. I couldn't talk to Conrad or the kids about this as I did not want to worry them more. I had an upcoming appointment with the breast screen clinic early May, so I put this worry to the back of my mind.

Sunday, April 14, we got to take Conrad out of the unit. I decided on a park very close to the facility, so I could take him back if he struggled or we needed help. We packed up a picnic lunch and headed to the water for two hours of family time. It was nice to spend time outside the facility and as a family. The kids loved it, and so did Conrad. Two hours were enough stimulation for the brain, and we had him back at the RU for a well-earned sleep for the rest of the afternoon. The kids headed home, and I picked up with my usual afternoon routine. It was a very long day for me but a step closer to home.

Our first family outing.

I had started to take more notice of his dreams and thoughts over the weeks, and it became apparent to me that he had a delayed reaction in processing what was in his mind and the conversations we had or places we'd been. One Saturday I noticed that he felt he was in jail. The next day he was in a boat on the water. When I analysed these thoughts, I realised the conversations we had the day before tended to be similar to where he thought he was the next day. I had discussed jail with him on the Friday, and that Saturday he felt he was in jail. We took him to the water Saturday, and Sunday he thought he was with water. I mentioned this to our children, so we were very mindful of the conversations we had to ensure he didn't have nightmares or put false thoughts into his mind.

I started to monitor this closer and noticed over the coming weeks his mind was actually doing this. I took him over to Starbucks for a coffee. By the time we got back to his room, he saw the lift in his eyes. As the days went by, his processes seemed to be getting closer. I mentioned this to his physio, and she paid attention to how he described his surroundings. Within a few days, she suggested I could be on to something. We would take him for a walk, and on returning to his room, he saw a rock wall. Or she would have him walk up and down the stairs, and by the time we got back to the gym area, he was seeing stairs. It was amazing to see his journey, and this fascinated me. I tended to watch him and his behaviours more, and I noticed daily the images were getting closer to the actual time they were experienced.

Each day he progressed with his walking (assisted) and going longer distances. Prior to his arrest, Conrad would ride twenty kilometres a day and go to the gym three or four times a week. He struggled with knowing what he thought he was capable of but couldn't remember. We had to continually remind him of how far he had come and not what he had lost in the way of his abilities. After the initial prognosis and ninety days in, every day was a great day in my books. And it still is.

Conrad often struggled with down moods. This was something I was very mindful of and something I felt in him when I arrived. My career direction of being an alternate life coach also helped. I had the ability to manage these in our conversations and encouraging him to think differently. The nurses often commented on this and were very supportive of Conrad, and any expressed thoughts or suggestions I put forward to help him with his tasks and moods were accepted wholeheartedly.

For Easter 2019, we got a day pass to take Conrad home. I decided Good Friday and Easter Sunday we would go home and have a break in the middle. I wasn't sure whether he would willingly return to hospital after his home visit, so I did up a contract for him to sign. Tony thought this was hilarious, especially at the wordings. He suggested we may need a tranquiliser dart if Conrad refused to return. Conrad signed the contract after a good laugh and finally agreeing to its terms. Mind you, he did take his time.

The long drive home was very tiring for him. I had him sit in the back seat to reduce the overwhelming effects of oncoming traffic and the city. I asked the kids to distract him during the drive, so he didn't have to focus on where we were going. We quickly popped in for a surprise visit with my brother and his family and then home for the day. By 2 p.m., Conrad started to get a little agitated, and I could see him getting stressed. I suggested I take home back to the hospital and get him settled prior to the 5:30 meal there. Much to my surprise, he was keen to return. After his meal and shower, he was ready to go to bed. It had been a huge day.

On Easter Saturday, I had to head to the Sunshine Coast for the morning to finish off some paperwork for a client. It was a further thirty minutes on top of my normal run. I had told Conrad that I needed to head north and would be at the hospital by about 1 p.m. I received nine calls in the space of an hour to see where I was. He had forgotten after each call. I told him to keep an eye out for "bunny ears." When I arrived at the hospital, I had my ears on and snuck around his door to the biggest smile when he saw them. We handed out chocolates to the other patients and an extra set of ears to one of the other patients that I had a soft spot for. Such a small gesture put so many smiles on the patients' and staff faces. It was lovely and very much worth it.

Easter 2019.

After such a big weekend, both Conrad and I were very tired. The next workday I got a phone call on the way to the hospital. I was not in the mood for attitude. According to him, he was sick of me only visiting every couple of days. He was sick of not having therapies, and he was pissed off at being left there to lie in a bed all day. Huh? Don't ever piss off a woman, especially a tired one. When I arrived—and now with my cranky pants on—he didn't see it coming. I dragged his backside around the building (meeting his new personal best) and had him do extra physio. I just happened to have my yoga pants on and sneakers, and he felt I had set him up. Nope. "You started this with your phone call," I let him know. He managed to sleep very well that night.

We had a home assessment on April 25, another step towards getting him home. The assessment went well, with only minimal modifications needed to be done at home, nothing major enough to hinder the discharge from hospital. Home time was getting closer.

On May 3, our guitar buddy Kevin was discharged. This brought about mixed emotions for all of us. Kevin had been a great support for Conrad, and I loved our jam sessions. Conrad was very down once he left, but I dragged his sad ass to the dining hall to kick it at Yahtzee and UNO. I had to make the most of a win somehow. He was also given his first weekend pass with a sleep at home. Yeah! The number of times over the weeks he had assured me that if he was in his own bed he would sleep well, ummmm, no way. We both got very little sleep as he tossed and turned. I had no idea how he lifted himself up so high off the bed at each turn. Along with needing to go to the toilet every hour. And when he did finally fall asleep, the nightmares kicked in. It was a long night for us both, although Conrad had no memory of it the next day. He just knew he was tired.

Tuesday, May 7, was the next meeting for Conrad to be discussed at the weekly conference call between facilities. I had hoped for his original **AROC** date of June 18, to be brought forward. (**AROC**- is the Australasian Rehabilitation Outcomes Centre. It is the national rehabilitation clinical registry of Australia and New Zealand. It contains all personal data and progress of any rehabilitation to establish a guideline to progress along with an expected date of discharge).

He had done so well in his therapy sessions and after consultation between myself and the social worker, and taking into account my feedback on how I would adjust at home as his fulltime carer, his discharge date was bought forward by four weeks! When the doctor told us, we both burst into tears. We could see a light at the end of the tunnel. It was unheard of at the unit for a patient to have their date brought so far forward. Most patients were pushed further back rather than brought closer. This was very exciting—and scary.

The next week had me filling out paperwork to support his National Disability Insurance Scheme (NDIS—government assistance for disability services) to enable support at home for a wheelchair, home modifications, and therapies. This was very confronting as it had to be broken down to every minor detail, such as he still needed assistance showering, toileting, walking, and eating, and so much more. It really hit me quite hard when it was broken down to such an extent. I had mixed emotions. I was so happy my husband was coming home, but this meant I was resigning from my role of financial controller and about to step into the role of my husband's full-time carer. I was worried about our relationship as well. Conrad was first and foremost my husband and had often commented on what was normal in our relationship and intimacy. I didn't want to have our relationship become patient/carer. This is something I am still very mindful of, even as I write this book. I also have to take into consideration how any activity we do, whether it be personal or physical, needs to take into account his abilities, heart, and health.

Along with the new changes about to happen, I was pending my check-up for the lumps I found earlier in my breast. I had advised the physio I would be late to his next session due to my own tests. When I arrived at his session, Conrad was not a very happy camper as I was late. I was used to biting my tongue. I knew he had no understanding or memory for him to realise his outbursts. I had seen this behaviour on several occasions. This is something that goes with an acquired brain injury and often doesn't get seen by visitors as he is distracted socially when they are with him. Thankfully, I got the all clear on the lump at that appointment with a follow-up later this year. The last six months had certainly been a roller coaster of emotions for us all. But we were now down to fewer than two weeks before Conrad was to come home.

Family time is always very special.

Wednesday, May 15, 2019, I arrived at the hospital to a very cranky patient. Conrad had been moved out of his room and into one with three other patients. He was tired after a morning visit from his parents, and he did not like the change to another room. I tried to explain to him this could be for several reasons, such as needing the room for a higher-needs patient, or the doctors may have been testing how he coped with change. At dinner he was very vocal about this until he heard another patient screaming and yelling. He looked horrified by all the noises coming from his old room, until I told him, "That was you ten weeks ago." He did not agree with that comment, so I grabbed one of the nurses who had been there for his journey. She confirmed this, and we both explained to him some of the nightly journeys she had with him—the camping trips, the car rides, packing the car, and the crocodiles. He did find the funny side as we told many stories of his journey. After dinner I returned him to his new room, and he was quietly accepting of the change and settled well after a shower. Taking into account his weekend home pass, he was down to four more sleeps in hospital. This was getting very exciting for him.

The last four days in the unit came and went, and the kids took the day off to pick Dad up from hospital. We celebrated with a family lunch and all looked forward to having our family back together for new beginnings.

Home time, yeah!

Encore

As with any good stage show or act, you need an encore. I can't say, in this instance, that it was bought on by applause or requested by the audience (ourselves), but I believe the universe again stepped in to give me closure on an unfinished situation.

Conrad was released from hospital Tuesday, May 21, 2019. After much excitement, the family was ready for the next stage in our journey. Little did we expect him to present with chest pains on Wednesday, only one day after coming home. No. To say we were a bit worried is an understatement. An ambulance was called, and after the paramedics assessed him and I updated them on his previous cardiac history, they did not hesitate in taking him straight to H1 for further evaluations.

I followed in the car and arrived at the hospital about ten that night. He was admitted to the emergency department, where testing started immediately in the way of blood tests and scans on the heart. It was a very long night. At 4 a.m., and after much pushing by me, a CT scan was done on his lungs and upper-left side to rule out any further blood clots, as that was what put him in hospital back in January. All tests came back clear, which was confusing for the doctors. He was moved to a ward at eight that morning and was to wait for the senior specialist to give him the all clear. There was a delay in finding his original medical files, and the lack of memory and understanding only compounded Conrad's emotional stresses. Mid-afternoon, the junior doctor arrived and advised he did not have the authority to release a patient. Conrad would be assessed by his senior before the end of day, all in the hope of being released today.

I had an uneasy feeling and requested a specialist nurse to be put on call if Conrad was to remain in hospital overnight. If he was to stay in, he could not be left alone for his own safety. The AIN arrived at 3 p.m. for her shift, and much to her delight, Conrad was her patient from back in February. She was very happy at how far he had come. We had a lovely chat and discussed Conrad's progress throughout his journey.

At 4 p.m. I requested a status update on the senior specialist. I was advised the doctor worked until after 6 p.m., and it was not unusual for rounds to be done into the early evening, and all with the intention of going home by the end of the day. By seven, Conrad was getting very distressed, and we were both very tired. I again called for an update, and at eight, the junior doctor arrived to tell us the senior had left. This brought both of us to tears as I knew I had to leave Conrad there overnight, in a hospital bed, with no understanding of the situation and why he was there. I left absolutely devastated for my husband. I was absolutely exhausted, having not eaten and still in my pjs from the previous night.

By eight the following morning, I was back at the hospital to do it all again. The same junior doctor arrived to tell us the same as the day before, and this time, he hoped to have Conrad discharged by lunchtime. We could work with that.

By 11 a.m., there was still no assessment by the senior. The junior again advised he did not have the authority to discharge but assured us that it shouldn't be too much longer. I followed up at five that afternoon. The same junior doctor returned to Conrad and advised we could go home. I thanked the doctor for his time, and we were finally on our way at six with the report I had requested.

What did I learn from the last two days?

Patience, maybe.

After reading through the report, I learned Conrad has minimal coronary heart disease in the remaining arteries. He has damage to the left ventricle chamber, and if we continue on optimal heart treatment for blood pressure and cholesterol, and he takes blood thinners, we should be able to manage this. Along with the previous ultrasounds at H2 in May, clearing artery blockages on either side of the throat, we are in a fairly good place and very lucky. This was all just the heart.

The brain, well that is a different journey. Conrad has a long, slow recovery ahead of him, but with the support and team he has, I know he will continue to progress and amaze his doctors and family around him. I also feel the universe stepped in to give me closure and help me not worry so much about the remaining arteries. Don't get me wrong, I still worry. But I make sure we are managing what we can through his medicine and his increased fitness and cardio health.

I have also learned to slow down and come back to present and be in the moment. I am very much—and always have been—aware of what *may* happen or what may need to be done moving forward, I acknowledge it and quickly come back to present.

I have threatened Conrad that the party trick and stage show we have been a part of for the last five months has had its encore moment and applause, and that is it! We will not be requesting or encouraging a further act.

Summary

As in my opening comments, "Everything is a foundation for something." I just didn't realise it at the time.

I believe the universe had me step back with my emotions for the months leading up to this event. This enabled me not to run on so much emotion when I needed more logic. I also believe that with Conrad opening up the last two weeks before he went down, it was enough to give him insight into what was available in a nonlogical sense for him to be open to receiving when needed. I feel these two things created a strong foundation to build upon and has gotten us to where we are today.

For 124 days, I wrote a daily poem for Conrad, I sent daily updates to friends and family on his progress, and I took photos and videos of his journey. I am very glad I did as these will be his memories until he can find his own. I have many hours of video moments with lots of love, tears, and laughter.

I have been told that I was a major contributing factor to his heart attack. I do not hold guilt in this space. Conrad was fully aware and in control of his signs prior to going down. And for five days, he did not seek medical advice, even after many requests from others and me. As noted previously, the two weeks prior to his cardiac arrest, we were in a beautiful place. That is what I hold on to and hope we will get back to in time.

Three months home, and as I finalise this manuscript, I can proudly say:

> My husband amazes me daily with his determination and fight to recover.

> He is walking, talking, feeding himself, and toileting and showering himself for the most part. He has jumped on the riding lawnmower and driven around his much-loved lawn. We go for breakfast and coffee dates on a weekly basis, and he loves to go to the beach. I am so grateful for his strength and recovery, and more thankful I fought as hard as I did in the early days. Contrary to professional advice early on, he has a very good quality of life, and this improves daily.

> The memory is slowly coming back. I have no doubt with his determination and the assistance we have on an energetic level, it will get better as the neuropathways reconnect and strengthen. He has a childlike innocence about him, and this comes out in his humour and his often-unfiltered comments. My husband is still very much in there; he just doesn't have the walls up. He even laughs out loud now, which is beautiful to hear and see.

> His quilt takes pride of place at the end of our bed, and he uses this in his daily naps.

He still struggles to sleep through the night. We are up at least three times each night. He still has nightmares, and oddly enough, they tend to be around car accidents. He has never been involved in an accident, so I have no idea where these come from.

We recently had a small storm pass over, and this had a minor effect on his brain and sensitivities, but they were manageable. We will see how we go over time and as storms increase toward summer.

We both recognise the signs of fatigue in him. His speech starts to slur, his vision gets blurry, and his left side shuts down when he gets tired. We have found a good balance, for the most part, in him having a daily nap of an hour or two. If he has big days with lots of stimulation and gets too exhausted, it can take him up to three days to recover from the lethargy and exhaustion. This is called a "fatigue hangover." His therapists have given him the description of his body having its own "fuel tank," and we check in on this during the day. When he gets towards half a tank, he knows to fill up by resting. I am very aware of his body language and adjust our activities accordingly.

I would not wish this journey on anyone, but I can honestly say I have learnt so much in this whole process. I have learnt so much about the brain, the unexplainable, and about myself. I have learnt to appreciate the valuable time we have and to make the most of our loved ones.

I have always had a positive attitude towards anything that life has thrown at me. I look for what I can learn and what I can change within myself. I am very much looking forward to the next chapter in our journey.

As with my weekly visits to my energy doctor on the Gold Coast, I equally look forward to working in the space of quantum and remapping the neuropathways with another energy healer that I met in October 2018 at the empath workshop. Watch this space!

If you ever find yourself in this kind of situation, strap yourself in cos you are in for one hell of a ride.

Remember to always find your balance in both emotion and logic.

And most of all,

Find your sense of humour!

124 DAYS OF POETRY

as I Ran through the Motion!

1.19.19

As I sit writing another poem,
I'm looking forward to the day you come home.
I know we have a challenge and a long road ahead.
But Babe, no matter what, I need you back in my bed.
I thought about starting with "Hickory, Dickory, Dock,"
But we all know that's yours and usually end with "My …"
So roses are red, violets are blue
Is another starter in my poem just for you.
I love you with all my heart,
And this is a chance for a new start.
So get your chatter monkeys in check to shut the f&ck up
Cos if they can't set you straight, I'll find a big truck.
You have an amazing network right by your side,
And just like before, we're all in for the ride.
As I've stated previously in our last plight,
Find your sense of humour cos we're in for one hell of a fight.

1.20.19

Well, today's 20 January 2019, and you
guess it—yup, another poem.
No different than yesterday, Bub, we need you at home.
I'm trying really hard to stay nice and strong.
It gets so hard at times cos you're not home where you belong.
I know it's only been a few days, and the doctors said to wait.
But I hate seeing you like this, and not
having you home we all hate.
A glimmer of hope yesterday for the kids and me.
You thought before my thoughts surprised you,
and this one you'll say I'm definitely crazy.
While in the shower, a visit from Dad,
Came a vision so strong, she wasn't sure what she had.
A call from Aunty Lee Lee with her thoughts just like mine,
"Get the quilt you made; we still have time."
The ball's in your court, Bub, you need
to find the strength tonight
To find the fight you need; the family
has heard your soul's plight.

1.21.19

Hey, Bub, headed to day 4,
And you still haven't walked through the door.
We thought before the family was put to the test.
But boy, oh boy, this is nothing compared to the rest.
It's hard seeing you try fight.
But this time, "You're not right."
All I ask is for you to focus on your breath.
I promise, Bub, to leave it up to the rest.
I love you with all my heart.
You need to come home for a new start.

1.22.19

Hey, Bub, you are still my loving Hub.
I got my sneakers on today
To tackle what you throw my way.
We had a good laugh at the shoe store,
But I had no idea what these sneakers were for.
With bright yoga pants on
And playing in my heart a sad song,
I'll put my big-girl smile on my face.
You know I don't exercise, but I'm in for your race.

1.23.19

Day 6, so long but so quick.
And my Bub is still in the ICU, very sick.
I'm trying my best to stay nice and strong,
But sometimes the challenges seem so wrong.
I've often said, "The bigger the hurt, the bigger the heal."
And know when I see you that "Yes, it's real."
So rest up, baby, and take your time
Cos I know as you do this, you will be back as mine!
I love you with all my heart and might.
Have no doubt, Bub, I won't go down without a fight.

1.24.19

Hey, baby, a whole week has gone,
and still we don't have you back home.
I've just climbed into bed at 10 o'clock.
I miss you, baby, you are our family rock.
I'm tired and exhausted and headed to bed.
Each day I try wake up with a clear head.

1.25.19

Hey, Bub, how ya doin'?
We're trying to get through to you.
Oh, wait, that's a song.
I'm doing a poem.
So day 8 and a little glimmer of hope.
You've given me something to help cope.
Chantelle called all excited; you finally blinked.
Just once, but it bought a tear when I winked.
A little step forward every day
says to me you want to stay.
I'm so proud of you and letting go.
I love you with all my heart and needed you to know.
So a little cheer from me
at each step forward we see.
The sneakers are on again for the marathon.
Bring it on, baby, we are on!

1.26.19

Hey, Bub, my loving hub.
Today I'm writing from the garden.
I'm looking at my veggies, thinking, *You need to harden.*
The feathered, two-legged ladies
run towards dinner daily.
Not much left of the veggie plot.
Actually, tomatoes and chilles, that's the lot!
The lettuce, sanchoy, and chives
fill the bellies of the 2-legged beady eyes.
I laugh each time they are the winner
cos our veggies and salad are their dinner.
I look up to the beautiful blue sky
and say to myself, "Do not cry.
He's safe and sound and needs to rest.
Today is just another test."
I'm so proud of you and the progress so far.
Know if I'm not with you, I'm never far.
You have your quilt and a direct line.
And know in time you'll be home and mine.

1.27.19

Hey, baby, I'm lying on our bed, resting up.
Getting some energy to go see my hub.
I'm trying to get through the daily grind,
but I can't seem to get you off my mind.
I hate seeing you in this state
cos, Bub, you are my soul mate.
It hurts like hell to see you struggle,
when all I want is a great big cuddle.
Rest up, baby, tomorrow's another day.
I pray to God you're progressing our way.

1.28.19

Hey, baby, we need you like mad.
Seeing you lying there helpless makes me so sad.
Every day I get up with fresh hope,
looking for something to help us cope.
We love you with all our heart and soul.
I need you to fill your "energy bowl."
You have so many loving friends.
The support you have never ends.
You are respected, loved, and adored,
and the kids and I have so much more.
Rest up, baby, and come back home.
I don't want to be without you and alone.
We love you to the moon and back.
Now get your shit back on track.
Said with love of course.

1.29.19

Hey, baby, another day you are resting.
I'm still smiling, but boy, you are testing.
I'm off to the Coast again today
to help your soul find its way.
How can you repair, heal, and mend
if you're out there floating to no end?
I'm trying with all my might
to give you the tools to help you fight.
I love you and want you back in my bed.
But I also understand it's time, they said.
So again, rest up, baby, come back to stay.
I'm doing my best to help you find your way.

1.30.19

Day 13, honey, and I'm not going away.
I'm doing all I can to help you stay.
But after much thought and consultation,
I've reassessed the sneaker "situation."
I've run my part for the last week and a half.
Now it's your turn to run some path.
I'll take on over at a later date.
I tell you now, it is our fate.
I'm handing over the baton in this marathon.
I'm saying, "Baby, your turn for a bit to carry on."
I'll be waiting with open arms in a short while
Looking at you with a great big smile.
You have got this, baby, I know you do.
I need you to know I do love you.

1.31.19

Day 14, babe, that's two weeks resting.
Everyday has challenges, some more testing.
I'm happy to say today you look content.
Time will tell to what extent.
I'm trying to find a balance and some "normal."
But you know me, we're not very formal.
The house is fairly tidy and somewhat clean.
But at the end of the week, cleaner I have seen.
The dogs miss you heaps, Nugget more so.
He's too docile to even know.
The veggie garden, we're not going to discuss.
All I can say is your chickens are guts.
The lawn we've seen greener.
But this dry weather has been meaner.
Rest yourself up, baby, and get well soon.
Just remember I love you to the moon.

2.1.19

Hey, baby, running into February now.
You keep this shit up, and I will turn into a cow.
Fifteen days and still counting.
The worry and concern are mounting.
We love you dearly and want you back,
but realise you need to make this track.
We miss you madly and love you so much.
I miss your smile and your tender touch.
I love you with all my heart and need you to know
I need you back for our love to grow.
Thirty years is not to be sneezed at.
I want to grow old with you and get grey and fat.
So rest up, baby, just take it slow.
I love you with all my heart, and I just want you to know.

2.2.19

Hey, baby, day 16.
Where have you been?
Oh, that's right, out there in space.
Apparently this is not a race.
I've been worried about your Celsius,
and it's hard cos you can't tell us.
I'm watching you closely to ensure you're okay.
That's part of why I'm here every single day.
The nurses here are doing a great task.
And for you to get better is all I ask.
We miss you like mad.
You're the best hubby I could have had.
Come back home where you belong.
I'll even sing you a very new song.
I'll start writing it now as you progress.
But don't go backward and start to regress.
We love you with all our heart.
Come on, baby, this is an exciting new start.

2.3.19

Hey, Bub, my loving hub.
Day 17, I'm starting to get scared
no matter how hard I try to show I cared.
You're slipping away day by day,
and no matter what, I can't make you stay.
It's so hard to watch you go.
But I love you with all my heart and need you to know
our life together has been such a gift,
and very rare did we have a rift.
A gorgeous home and three amazing kids,
I still reflect on your amazing gifts.
You've been a friend, a lover, and my life,
I just hope you know I'm a very proud wife.
No matter how hard I try to make you stay,
in the end it's your choice on your final day.
Thank you for all you are, have, did, and gave.
I will take your love to my dying grave.
So rest up, baby, and do what you must.
In the universe and our love I need to trust.
I will do my best to laugh out loud
and my utmost to make you proud.

2.4.19

Hey, baby, day 18, and I'm feeling numb.
I sit here and wonder, *How could we be so dumb?*
The signs were there but we just dismissed.
I kick myself; I'm really pissed.
You knew for five whole days,
but as usual, the control had its ways.
I sit here now, watching you in the bed,
And each day I'm starting to dread.
It's so hard to see you struggle,
and all I want is a heartfelt snuggle.
I miss you more than you'll ever know.
And yes, I'm selfish; I don't want you to go.
Just remember I love you so much
and miss you every day and your loving touch.
Rest up, baby, try and restore.
Just know always I love you more!

2.5.19

Hey, Bub, day 19, and you're nearing the end.
I dread when I think what's around the next bend.
I'm hurting so much, and it pains me to see.
I wish you had just listened; you'd still be here with me.
We tried so hard to give you the tools,
but I sit and wonder, *Who's the bigger fool?*
Your stubborn attitude will take you to your grave.
It wasn't enough, no matter how much I gave.
You often said I defied you at all cost.
But babe, I never gave up cos our love was not lost.
I don't generally carry anger as an emotion,
but I tell you now it's running through the motion.
I'm sad, I'm lonely, and I'm being torn apart
cos every day I lose you more; it's breaking my heart.
I love you more than I could ever say,
so in a poem I write it every day.
Rest up, baby, and do what you must.
In God, the angels, and the universe I must trust.

2.6.19

Hey, baby, day 20, and I'm not going away.
I still hope you can find the will to stay.
The doctors and nurses are doing a great job,
but you are being such a flog.
It's nice to see you're more relaxed today.
It helps me to see that you're okay.
We love you lots and always will.
I still can't swallow this bitter pill.
Rest up, baby, take your time.
I love you heaps; you're always mine.

2.7.19

Day 21, three weeks and counting.
I can tell you, babe, the pressure's mounting.
Today you looked so peaceful sleeping,
while at your bedside I sit keeping.
I'm bursting with pride and love you so much,
and know the angels and God I still trust.
I just hope all infection stays away
to give you rest for another day.
I'm sending you big hugs and lots of energy
cos I'd love nothing more than to have you back with me.
Rest up, baby, I want you to know
I love you with all my heart, and it's hard to let you go.

2.8.19

Hey, baby, day 22,
and we still love you.
I'm so proud of your efforts to date.
And the gradual progression, I cannot wait.
You're starting to confuse the hell out of all.
And believe me, I still hear your call.
You actually spoke to me yesterday.
The doctors still aren't sure what to say.
In frustration and dragging from the bed,
"I wanna go home," is what you said.
I'm happy to sit and watch you recover,
and help defy medical logic and discover.
One day at a time is all I ask.
I know you have one hell of a task.
Rest up, baby, I love you more
And very much look forward to the day
you walk through the door.

2.9.19

Hey, baby, day 23, I'm not going away.
I'm doing all I can to help you stay.
I've battled, I've argued, I've fought for your cause
In the hope that one day you will walk through the door.
I can't say it's been easy to not start "bitch slappin'."
But as you come back to me, I start clapping.
The "negative Nancys" and constant naysayers
can all get stuffed cos you are a stayer.
I know you have strength, conviction, and pride.
I tell you now, babe, I'm in for the ride.
I know there's still a journey and a hell of a task,
but a little progress each day is all I ask.
I will not abandon you and leave your plight.
I've got your sneakers back on and am in for the fight.

2.10.19

Hey, baby, day 24, and I'm still stalking you.
Every day I get up with a somewhat positive view.
We're watering the garden and nourishing your mind,
all the time trying to be kind.
The sprinkler in on doing its tinkle,
and the grass is getting greener with the sprinkle.
The kids are doing awesome keeping it at bay,
looking forward to when you come back home to stay.
I love you with all my heart and cannot wait
for our Wednesday and weekend dinner dates.
Rest up, baby, and recover
cos when you get home, we can rediscover.

2.11.19

Hey, baby, day 25, and you still keep 'em guessing.
Every day I see you progress is another blessing.
Dr N is the new doctor today,
and I gotta say I love her ways.
She's bright and bubbly, and I think like me.
With her shoes, beads, and smile, I think she'd hug a tree.
She gave me a happy dance
and told me about this chance.
The drug they had you on
seems to have been so wrong.
On top of this I went to see Dr Alt.
As you know, I always like her alternate advise.
I think we've got all your bases covered,
and I cannot wait to watch you recover.
I love you lots and am so proud of you.
You need to come home; you are our family glue.

2.12.19

Hey, baby, day 26, and we're still hanging around.
I'm so proud of you and you standing your ground.
You've had a massive day with activities galore,
a trip to the café, shower, physio, and more.
You even managed to swallow some food,
which is huge progress; this is good.
One step at a time, and progress each day,
is a little bit closer to getting you home our way.
As I write today's poem, I'm trying to keep you awake.
You keep falling asleep at the poor nurse's sake.
I love you lots; you're doing awesome, Bub.
As always, you are still my loving hub.

2.13.19

Hey, baby, day 27 and our lucky number!
You are so tired but still won't slumber.
I call each morning to see how you slept.
But this morning, for you I could have wept.
You didn't sleep a wink, and you really should.
A good night's sleep will actually do you good.
How is your body to recover
if a sleep pattern you can't discover?
You finally drifted off at 4:30 p.m, today,
listening to Kip Moore country songs play.
You look so tired, and your body's worn.
My heart aches, and I feel so torn.
I wish I could fix this and make you heal.
We love you heaps and want you home for a meal.
Rest up, baby, and try to sleep.
Remember in our hearts, you we'll always keep.

2.14.19

Hey, baby, day 28, and its Valentine's Day.
I'm not going anywhere; I'm here to stay.
They moved you to a ward today.
I'm hoping this isn't a very long stay.
I'm worried, I'm concerned, I'm not impressed.
All I need you to do is rest!
I'm researching for the best rehab for you.
But it's still going to take a little time to do.
I need you to progress and not get sicker,
and rest and recover to gradually get better.
It breaks my heart to see you like this
cos, my loving hub, I do so much miss.
Rest up, baby, find your strength.
I will do what I can and will go to great length.
I love you lots; you are my soul mate.
To get you back home I cannot wait.

2.15.19

Hey, baby, day 29, and you're progressing slowly.
I miss you at home; sometimes it's so lonely.
They are talking about your progress so far.
I'm so proud of you, you're my shining star.
We hate seeing you like this and wish we could make it better.
And every day I write it in a letter.
You're doing amazing, babe.
I tell everyone; I even rave.
I love you with all my heart.
Come home soon, baby, for our new start.
Rest up, baby, and get yourself right.
It won't be long 'til you're home all night.

2.16.19

Hey, baby, day 30 and Liam's eighteenth birthday.
We miss you at home and want you back our way.
You mustn't yet be sick of your daily poem
cos if you were, you'd be back home.
You're progressing each day, and we are so proud of you
It's times like these you know our love is true.
You're not sleeping of a night, and you're absolutely exhausted.
But then I come to visit, and you sleep peacefully in your bed.
I watch you quietly as you are resting.
I gotta say, the last month has been very testing.
But babe, every day I come to visit you,
I am amazed at your determination and you pushing through.
So again, rest up, baby, you're doing marvellous.
I know in time you'll be back with us.

2.17.19

Hey, baby, day 31, and we're still around.
We are watching you daily to see you homeward bound.
I feel you are going to kick some ass
and get yourself home real fast.
Your fight and determination surprise us all.
You've done amazingly every day since your fall.
You've shown us how to fight and not give up.
And at the end, we will raise to you an alcoholic cup.
We miss you at home and know this is still a task.
But you getting better is all we ask.
So take your time, baby, and rest all you can.
I know it won't be long, and you will be home again.

2.18.19

Hey, baby, my loving hub, day 32.
I'm sitting here lonely and missing you.
Big day today with the Coast and a call on the way.
I'm praying like mad we can get you to the next stage.
They say it's the best rehabilitation for you.
And if I have my way, I will do all I can do.
I'll contact the local member, if I need.
And as many phone calls just to plead.
We want you back home and love you so much.
I miss you like mad and want your hubby touch.
Rest up, baby, let yourself rest.
I've still got your back in this challenging test.

2.19.19

Hey, baby, day 33 and another poem.
I'm looking forward to the day you come home.
We miss you like mad and hope you get well.
We love you with all our heart and hope you can tell.
You mean the world to us, and we are so proud of you.
I hope you know how much the kids and I love you.

2.20.19

Hey, baby, day 34, and you're progressing each day.
I'm hoping not too long before you are back home our way.
The days are long, and it's hard fitting it all in.
And some days I wonder, but I am having a win.
Mum's gone home as she is not well.
When she'll back, I cannot tell.
We're managing along
and trying to stay strong.
I'm looking forward to you coming home.
I'm being selfish; I don't want to sleep alone.

2.21.19

Hey, baby, five weeks that you've been in this bed.
As each day passes, I have less dread.
You're slowly regaining your strength and memory.
I know it's only time 'til you're back with me.
You're not sleeping or getting much rest.
Which, I am sure, puts the nurses to a test.
I'm sitting here at four o'clock; you are at rest.
I am glad for you as sleep is the best.
To rest your brain and help you recover
And when you wake, I'm eager to discover.
Yesterday your job was a property developer.
In your mind you were in meeting, had land, and was a seller.
I did have a giggle when Liam called.
Apparently we interrupted, and your meeting stalled.
The look of disgust, and you showed your class,
as your comment to me was, "You're a fxxxing smart ass."
We laugh with you as you progress.
Sleep tonight, Bub, you need your rest.

2.22.19

Hey, baby, day 36; you're now in a four-bed room.
You're progressing towards rehab, and
each day there's less doom.
They've changed up your meds to find you a balance.
And you're settling more, so it's less of a challenge.
Before you know it, you will be off for the next stay,
and I will be so happy when we know that day.
It's a brain injury unit for your type of heart attack.
And it's a fast rehabilitation to get you back.
I know with your determination and your fight
this place is the one for you; it's just right.
On a positive side, and with the move to it,
you'll be doing rehab, and so is Billy Pitt.
He went down himself, before you, and damaged his spine.
And just like you, doctors say it will take time.
Rest up, baby, we love you lots.
I love your fight, progress, and guts.

2.23.19

Hey, bay, day 37 as I sit beside your bed.
I smile so proudly cos sleep helps your head.
You're starting to find a balance in your
journey moving forward.
And every good day with rest is a little step toward.
Your little grins and dry humour we do laugh at.
And we know each day we slowly get you back.
We still have a journey and an unknown task.
But the brain injury rehab unit is your next path.
Four hours a day minimum intense rehab
will get you strong, like the dad we had.
Rest up, baby, and relax your mind.
We are 100 per cent with you and have your behind.

2.24.19

Hey, baby, day 38 and a Sunday.
Hopefully, you will be home some, someday.
We miss you like mad, and it's lonely at home.
It's hard leaving you at hospital to come home alone.
I know you are fighting hard to come back to us.
With almost six weeks down, your strength I must trust.
I've never given up or forgotten your plight.
Every day I get up, for you I will fight.
I love you with all my heart and want you with me.
You are the glue in our loving family.

2.25.19

You guessed it, another poem at day 39.
I'm still waiting patiently for you to be mine.
A little step back today in your imagination.
Seems the opiate you're now off caused hallucination.
Throw in the possibility of an infection as well
has me watching you a little closer, just so I can tell.
A trip to Dr Alt again was a long drive in the car.
But for you and your health, babe, I drive that far.
Again, the naysayers can doubt all they like
cos for you and your body, I know this is right.
I'm learning myself and trusting the universe above.
And I know over time you'll come back to us, my love.
So sleep and rest up, baby, let your brain recover.
Over time and rehab our love we'll rediscover.

2.26.19

Hey, baby, day 40, and a huge day for you.
Physio, speech, and nutrition too.
Every day you impress us more.
I smile every day I walk through the door.
Your determination, will, and fight
will have you back home soon of a night.
Keep progressing, Bub, and getting stronger.
I don't think you will be here too much longer.

2.27.19

Hey, baby, day 41, and I'm here again.
I'm here every day, doing all I can.
You're getting better with your conversation,
but your mind runs off late daily with imagination.
They call it "sundowners," and it confuses you
cos in your mind, you see it as true.
You've been in meetings and a property developer.
You've been a builder and a business manager.
You've been relaxed and cranky as shit.
You've been chatting but also ready to hit.
Every day is a different day, and I'm not sure what to expect.
I'm not sure how you will react.
Our family is strong, and we'll get through it all.
I understand this is your journey and your soul's call.
We've got your back and are in for this journey.
I know it's only time 'til you're back with the kids and me.

2.28.19

Hey, baby, day 42, oh, what a day.
Today has been hard, and I'm not sure what to say.
It's an understatement to say today was a test.
But basically, it all started with a night of no rest.
The lady opposite screamed all the night.
This, I'm sure, for you was a horrid fright.
I got a call at 9 a.m. from Pablo
to see if I could settle you for your physio.
You managed to do all that was asked.
But by 2 p.m., well, that was another task.
I arrived at your bed, and you were in a state of panic,
with doctors and nurses all around manic.
It broke my heart, and I ran to your side
to calm and soothe you and regain your pride.
They finally recognised your brain's overstimulated
and moved you to a quiet room to be rehabilitated.
So rest up. baby, I hope tonight you are sound.
And I wish for you no noise or stimulation to be found.

3.1.19

Hey, baby, day 43 and now into March.
The last six weeks have been such a task.
Your new room has given you a rest.
Now for the rehab team to put you to the test.
I met your speechie, your physio, and the quack.
This awesome team is going to help get you back on track
in full consultation with the social team.
I'm looking forward to your progress as you redeem.
You have amazed me daily with your asks.
And even going to the toilet is an eventful task.
I'm so proud of you and the strength you have shown.
I know in my heart that in time you will be home.
Rest up, baby, and get more muscle
cos the physio team on Monday will make you bustle.

3.2.19

Hey, baby, day 44, and I'm still here.
Every day I let out a little cheer.
You've shown our kids determination and fight.
And me challenging the doctors was absolutely right.
You have no idea on how I burst with pride
cos it's not always been a fun ride.
You have struggled and hurt and pushed through.
And, babe, I have to say we are so proud of you.
Keep going as you are and plodding along.
I know one day soon you will be nice and strong.

3.3.19

Hey, baby, day 45 and the end of a weekend.
The days are so long and never seem to end.
You feel you have strength and can stand by yourself.
But believe me, Bub, you still need help.
Your mind says you are able,
but you fell and hit your head on the table.
One step at a time is what it will take,
and lots of rehab for a stronger you to make.
Get a decent night's sleep, Bub.
And remember, you are my loving hub.

3.4.19

Day 46, Bub, we're both getting tired.
But my love for you will never expire.
You have new challenges with your therapy,
and every day it brings you closer back to me.
I love you lots, and you're doing great.
Please get a good night's sleep and not stay up late.
Sleep well, baby, I miss you like mad.
Sleeping by myself makes me sad.

3.5.19

Hey, baby, day 47 and a good day.
Every day a step closer to coming home to stay.
You've had occupational therapy, and she challenged you
to touch your nose and knees to learn anew.
You did amazing; I was really impressed.
In your new shorts and shirt, you were appropriately dressed.
You're very tired tonight, and you need a good night's rest.
I know again tomorrow the physio will put you to the test.
You stood on your own while leaning on a frame.
I'm really impressed, Bub, you are really on your game.
Rest up, baby, have a good night's sleep
cos every day there are new memories to keep.

3.6.19

Day 48, I should find a new start for my poem.
But this won't change, Bub: We want you back home.
Today has been a massive day.
You're getting a little closer to home and our way.
You're being moved finally to the rehabilitation unit, the RU.
I was very nervous but let out a little "Woohoo."
It's been a tiring and massive day.
But babe, guess what? You're at the PA.
One last leg of this challenging journey.
It won't be long, babe, 'til you're home again with me.

3.7.19

Seven weeks today, but who is counting?
I tell you, Bub, the pressure has stopped mounting.
Your first night at the PA was restful,
and from what the nurses say, you seemed to be peaceful.
I'm so excited and happy for you
cos Bub, you're at the RU!
Every day they are going to challenge you.
This is the facility that will get you through.
Thank you, baby, for trying with all your might
and sticking around during this hell of a fight.

3.8.19

Hey, honey, day 50 and a challenging start.
The third day at the RU, and they are
worried about your heart.
They took you off the opium patch last night.
It seems this had masked your pain from sight.
Not only did this drug give you hallucinations,
it had you believe what was in your imagination.
The pain that has been inside your chest
Was now putting the doctors to the test.
They all hit panic and checked your enzymes
They thought another heart attack was in line.
I conferred and tried to set them straight.
You've had the pain for years to date.
They cannot see how this is so,
and it put a stop to your physio.
A couple of days' rest will show you are strong,
and the initial thought was oh, so wrong.
I'm trusting my guidance and inner sense,
and I feel they are wrong about your inner strength.
Time will tell; I'm not stressing yet.
You'll show them wrong again, I can bet.
I love you, Bub, please don't stress.
I don't want you to put your heart under more duress.

3.9.19

Hey, Bub, day 51 and a Saturday.
I feel a long day is headed my way.
An early start in the city centre.
A fundraising boot camp for all to enter.
You know me, I don't exercise.
So my yoga mat in the middle of sweaty
bodies should be no surprise.
I laughed and giggled most of the time.
And your boss did, too, but with a bottle of wine.
Then off to visit you with Chantelle.
You were so exhausted; no sleep again, we could both tell.
We left at three as we had other commitments.
For the girl a party, and me, the Eagles
concert for some entertainment.
I missed you like mad and worried all night,
hoping you would rest, and you'd be all right.
Rest up, Bub, I hope you get some sleep.
It won't be long 'til you're home for keeps.

3.10.19

Hey, baby, day 52,
And I am soooo proud of you.
Today you read to me the signs we wrote
to help you with a mental note.
I put them on your wall to see,
and I read them to you at every opportunity.
But today your vision is coming back,
and day by day, you're getting back on track.
You scattered the sentences occasionally.
But babe, you did it, you did it, you read them to me.
I'm so proud of you and your efforts so far.
Babe, I gotta say, you are my biggest star.
Thank you for fighting and being so strong.
It won't be long 'til you are home where you belong.

3.11.19

Hey, baby, day 53, and what a day.
Today your mind has been way astray.
The hallucinations are scary as shit.
They have not let you rest, not one little bit.
You've thrashed and yelled and moved around.
You did all you could to walk on the ground.
I came intending a really good visit
but left upset and really not with it.
It broke my heart to see you so scared.
I wish you could see how much I cared.
I hope tonight is a better night,
and the dreams and drugs don't cause you fright.
I love you lots; I hope you sleep well, Bub.
Always remember you are my loving hub.

3.12.19

Hey, Bub, day 54, and I still got your back.
A good night's sleep will get you on track.
I'm feeling better today, Bub, you have got this.
I look forward to seeing you daily and giving you a kiss.
Your first real physio was today,
And you blew me away.
I reckon you walked half our backyard.
Your first attempt, Bub, must have been so hard.
You also called me at lunchtime to say you could read my signs.
Bub, you did, and as you read them, it blew my mind.
I am so grateful and love you so much.
Thank you, honey, for staying strong and being my hub.

3.13.19

Hey, honey, day 55, and you are going strong.
You will be home before you know it; it won't be long.
I had a meeting today with social worker Amy,
and I'm so excited at what she said to me.
We have some indication on your AROC date.
Bub, I've told the kids it's in June, and I can't wait.
I had a feeling all along, and before you went down,
that March and June were important for
something to come around.
In March you went to the RU, your final stepping stone.
And June is the next, and you will be home.
I have a further intuition; mid-May might now be it.
So I'm setting you the challenge for you to get fit.
I know you've got this, Bub, and you will give it a whirl.
Cos every time you have physio and slacken,
I tell you, "You bat like a girl!"

3.14.19

Eight weeks today, Bub, how can that be?
Every day is closer to having you back with the kids and me.
I'm so proud of you and want you to know
you surprise the crap out of me and also the physio.
After only two days up on your feet,
the distance you walked would be
equivalent to the end of our street.
Your determination, strength, and your fight,
I see in your eyes, Bub, you are trying with all your might.
I trust in you and know you will do your best.
And no different than before, you will
put your body to the test.

3.15.19

Hey, Bub, day 57 and another achieved mission.
You're now off the hoist and at two-person transition.
I watch you closely each day in the hope of getting you back.
The last thing we need is another heart attack.
Tonight while I played guitar and sang you a song,
I looked at you and knew something was wrong.
Your eyes, the pupils, they were two sizes to me.
You were very anxious and scared of the thunder activity.
This is so unlike you, to be scared at all.
Normally, you would stand in the
middle of a storm nice and tall.
You did have a giggle when I called you "floppa dog."
You said you could both lie together and shake and sob.
It's beautiful seeing you with some vulnerability.
And Bub, I'm looking forward to when you come home to me.

3.16.19

Hey, baby, day 58, and you are finally "getting it."
The processes need to be run, and you are digging in with grit.
Last night you were awake and all-around too.
Apparently you have strength. and we never knew.
You stood up alone in your bed
and tried to climb the wall at the nurse's dread.
You and I laughed at your daring plan,
especially when I asked, "Did you think you were Spiderman?"
You can't remember but took it in stride.
Bub, I look at you with love and with so much pride.
Every day you come up with something funny.
I love you with all my heart; you are my honey.

3.17.19

Hey, baby, two months today, but who's counting?
I'm relieved to say the pressure has stopped mounting.
Every day you are getting stronger.
But the days for me are getting longer.
I'm trying to find a balance in this chaotic life.
Babe, I would do this and more cos I am your wife.
Every day I see you as progressing.
It makes me smile, and you are impressing.
Keep it up, Bub, one day at a time.
Only a few more months, and you will be home and mine.

3.18.19

Day 60 in this life-learning journey.
Another day closer to coming home to the kids and me.
As with every other week up to now,
you find the strength; I don't know how.
I smile when I think of you being so strong
and the challenging journey that we have all been on.
I went to the Coast again today.
I still believe this is the way.
Dr Alt has been an amazing channel and a tool,
even if the family thinks I am a fool.
Every day you defy the medical profession.
And this, for me, has been an eye-opening lesson.
I love you, Bub, I truly do.
I have all faith that you will get through.

3.19.19

Hey, baby, day 61 still plodding along.
Every day I love you more; you're staying strong.
Another challenging day to your physical strength,
with OT, speech, and physio, all at great length.
You're finding your feet and standing tall.
Bub, I know you will be walking in no time at all.
I watch you daily with a very proud grin.
I have your back, babe, I am 100 per cent in.
Your mind is a worry and messing with your head.
It seems while everyone is sleeping, the
nightmares come you dread.
It's gunna take time to get you back on track.
But have patience, it won't be long until you are fully back.

3.20.19

Hey, baby, you'd be getting bored with my opening line.
But like day 1, we want you back; it will just take time.
You challenge yourself every single day.
I have no doubt you are here to stay.
Take your time, Bub, there's nothing for you to do but rest.
Being patient and listening is your biggest test.
The universe has got you on its side.
Every time I think of this, I burst with pride.
You are my soul mate, my lover, and my friend
Together we will be 'til the very end.

3.21.19

Nine weeks tonight, Bub, and that's okay.
Cos, baby, at this rate, you are here to stay.
Every day I walk through the door.
You greet me with a smile, a hug, and so much more.
Your strength, determination. and your fight
proves to me "our fight" was so right.
I'm so proud of you and what you have become.
You have so many fans, but I am your number 1.
Keep going ahead in leaps and bounds.
It won't be long now 'til you're homeward bound.

3.22.19

Hey, baby, it's day 63.
It won't be too much longer 'til you are home with me.
Step by step you progress each day.
I'm so proud of you, I'm happy to say.
You got on an exercise bike today for a quick pedal.
I was so impressed; you deserve a medal.
Your physio is impressed with your progress as well.
You are challenging her too, I can tell.
You're catching, you're throwing, and holding a stance.
Bub, I'm so excited; this is a second chance.
Keep on pushing through and giving it your best.
I have full faith in you; you will pass this test.

3.23.19

Hey, baby, day 64.
Another challenge today to test us a little more.
A distressed call to me in the early hours of the morning
left me worried; your heart sent a warning.
We still have concern and a few hurdles yet.
A date with the specialist needs to be set.
Chest pains, blood tests, and another X-ray
just to make sure nothing has gone astray.
You keep me on my toes, on this roller-coaster ride.
Each day I smile, and my fear I try to hide.
Two steps forward and one step back.
This seems to be the pace to keep you on track.
Stay strong, Bub, the kids and I are all by your side.
And just like day 1, we are in for this ride.

3.24.19

Hey, baby, day 65; I'm still tallying them up.
Yesterday I hit the beach to try fill my energy cup.
You have had a busy day with lots of social time,
including a visit from Dad and Sue, who
were impressed with your mind.
You and Chantelle challenged me today
and thought it was a joke.
Until the KFC chip you bullied me for caused you to choke.
You coughed and spluttered; I waited for
you to throw up in your bed.
I crapped myself and thought, *Speechie's*
gunna kill me; boy I am dead.
It was a big lesson learned, and next time I won't be so soft.
If it's outside Speechie's orders, I will tell you both to fxck off!

3.25.19

Hey, Bub, day 66 and almost through March.
Another sleepless night; boy, this is a task.
I think these stimulating days with lots going on
keep you up all night; it's sad and it's wrong.
I'm learning lots, Bub, especially about your brain,
from stimulation to storms and even the effects of rain.
Every day I see you progressing and growing.
I tell you now, in this journey, we are
both learning and knowing.
My guides and angels say I need to write and be teaching.
And this journey we are on, for others, will be far-reaching.
Time will tell, and it will be with your support.
Others will know just how hard we both fought.

3.26.19

Another big night and more chest pains.
This roller-coaster ride, I'm still holding onto the reins.
More X-rays, Nitrate, and another lot of blood tests,
along with less physio and more bedrest.
We need to find your balance and get you stable.
The physical will progress only as you are able.
Our family meeting says you're coming along well.
But the heart will take time for the specialist to tell.
You're now slowly walking and talking
and starting to feed yourself.
You should be so proud at how far you
have come with your health.
I'm looking forward to walking back into ICU
and showing them all what hope and love can do.
The kids and I never gave up the fight.
From day 1 I had you in my sight.
I love how hard you fought just to stay
and look forward to having you home very soon one day.

3.27.19

Day 68, and I reckon about halfway.
I'm hoping on the downhill run until you are home to stay.
A good night's sleep makes a huge difference,
and it seems the next day there is less sufferance.
You remembered your nurse today, which is a huge step ahead,
With a little progress we hope the
memories can stay in your head.
You're progressing each day, and it's awesome to see.
It won't be long, Bub, 'til you are home with the kids and me.

3.28.19

Day 69, and you are still not home.
The kids and I really miss you, and you are sleeping alone.
Today big steps forward with a pass out of the RU.
Andrew was first to have a cuppa with you.
I have to say he deserved it as a reward
cos in physio you used him as your target board.
You threw beanbags at his shoulder and his face.
And it wasn't long 'til you marked the right place.
We all laughed at the challenge we had set for you,
and true to Chatham form, you really shone through.

3.29.19

Hey, Bub, day 70 and another hiccup in your path.
It seems every time you move, you end
up dizzy and about to pass.
I've monitored your movement to see when you fall/
And the physio seems to think she might be on to it all.
You fell and hit your head very early on in RU.
You were way too quick for the nurse to assist you.
As you came down it seems your inner ear is now out of whack,
and the Dizzy Physie can hopefully help put you back on track.
It seems the bump on your head has now given you vertigo.
It will take time to see how you go.
A roll to the left and a quick move to your side
had you almost throwing up on this not so fun ride.
It will take a couple of days to see success,
and crossing fingers will lead to a good night's rest.

3.30.19

Day 71 and almost the end of another week.
More visitors yesterday had you too tired to sleep.
It was a lovely surprise to see your sister from interstate.
And you were very lucky to take the family on a coffee date.
It seems the more tired you are, the harder it is to sleep.
And when I come to visit you, I almost weep.
I try to keep it quiet when it's just you and me,
but I also understand it's nice for you to see family.
It's a roller-coaster ride to find you a rest,
and not everyone realises this is one of my biggest tests.
I hope you sleep tonight and store some energy.
This is what your brain needs to help with recovery.

3.31.19

Hey, baby, day 72, the last day of March.
I can't believe the time is going by so fast.
As from day 1, you amaze me each day.
It's always a positive step towards coming home to stay.
I love my daily visits and the smile that greets me.
And more so excited at the progress I see.
Keep staying committed, determined, and strong.
At this pace, you will be home, and it won't be too long.

4.1.19

Hey, Bub, day 73 and April Fool's Day.
Another Dizzy Physie to take the spins away.
It's not a funny joke when you're about to throw up.
You are so very tired with an empty energy cup.
I can't let you sleep or even lie down on your back
as the crystals now in place may fall back off the track.
It's hard to explain and try to tell it's all okay
cos no matter what we tell you, it doesn't seem to stay.
We feel for you, honey, and struggle by your side.
But, babe, as at day 1, we are all in for the ride.

4.2.19

Hey, Bub, day 74 and another rough night.
It's hard to understand what keeps giving you fright.
You seem to settle in the day, when I am sitting by your side.
But when I leave at night, it's a lot rougher of a ride.
The nurses can't seem to settle you as
what's in your mind seems real.
And when they call me in the night, my heart for you does feel.
Rest when I am there, if that's all you can manage.
Your brain needs rest to repair some of the damage.

4.3.19

Day 75, and we are running through the days.
Each day you have a therapy gets you closer to our way.
You are blitzing all the challenges the therapist sets for you.
And coming up with new tasks is what we try to do.
You caught a soccer ball today and
showed great muscle memory.
But to get the muscles back will take time for us to see.
You are doing great, Bub, and I couldn't ask for more.
I know it won't be long 'til you are walking through our door.

4.4.19

Eleven whole weeks you have not been in your bed.
But that's okay, Bub, we need to fix your head.
The brain is progressing slowly and doing all that it's asked.
No matter what we set you, you take on the task.
I am so proud of you and all the fight you show.
The kids and I are so grateful, I need you to know.
Rest up, Bub, and recover at your own pace.
There is no finish line in this never-ending race.

4.5.19

Another big day with lots of visitors at the RU.
A nice surprise with your mum and
dad, and aunt and uncle too.
I'm dreading the night ahead and how
many phone calls I will get
cos the nurses are not able to help settle
you in your hospital bed.
The memory is not retaining, and it's
making things hard for you.
But babe, there is no expectation, or line you need to get to.

4.6.19

Hmm, where do I start today? No sleep and a rough night.
Overstimulation, it's hard and doesn't seem right.
People keep telling me it doesn't come into play,
but I tell you now, you do not sleep after a big day.
I've really taken notice of your journey and your brain.
I've learnt so much, I'm excited to help you retrain.
We've been given a second chance and a big life lesson.
Going forward, with your health we won't be messing.
Another day down; I need you to rest.
The kids and I still know we are very blessed.

4.7.19

Hey, baby, day 80, and such a busy day you have had.
Lots of visitors, starting with your mum and dad.
Denis and Ros flew up to say hi as well.
You were very excited when I called; I could tell.
I'm trying to take lots of photos to create a memory book.
Your memory is not retaining, so at least when
you are home you can have a look.
It's extra hard for me and you
cos after busy days, you don't sleep at the RU.
The dreaded calls the nurses make to me at night,
wake me at all hours from my sleep with such a fright.
I feel so bad for you as you are so distressed.
I wish that you could just close your
eyes and sleep a peaceful rest.
I'm bracing myself for calls tonight and
expect it almost every hour.
I'll reassure you with my voice and all that is in my power.

4.8.19

Hey, baby, day 81 and another sleepless night.
At least there weren't as many calls to
wake we me with a fright.
You've had a very busy day with normal therapy,
but the doctors also booked you for an EEG.
The nurse, I had to laugh at; you really
surprised her and all by just talking.
But the look on her face was priceless when
I told her you were also walking.
After years and years of testing hypoxic
brains, she finally met you.
And Bub, I think you are her first patient who's not in the ICU.
I asked her about hypoxic brain injury
and her known statistics.
And the progress you have made to
date seems to be unrealistic.
I smile with pride when I explain our journey
and the challenges you endured to
come back to the kids and me.
Stay strong, Bub, and continue as you are.
You'll be home before you know it; it won't be that far.

4.9.19

Hey, baby, it's day 82.
And every day I am so proud of you.
Today during physio, Nicola thought she would challenge you.
And for the first time ever, she walked you
around the building of GARU.
You did awesome; it was a good 300 metres at least.
And by the time you got back, you said you had sore feet.
Every day you are going a little further.
And Bub, I have to tell you I couldn't be prouder.
I see it in your eyes, how hard you have to fight.
It won't be too much longer until you
are in your own bed at night.

4.10.19

Hey, baby, my phone rung off the hook last night.
At least five times you called and woke me with a fright.
You couldn't sleep, and the nurses struggled to reassure you.
All your yelling and frustration kept
the other patients awake too.
It's hard, Bub, cos you don't remember
even making a single call.
Even every hour, the memory you don't recall.
I lay in bed for ages, hoping you will fall asleep.
And wondering if at all, any memory you will keep.
On a positive note for today,
a little step closer to a home stay.
Your beloved Colorado I drove to RU.
This was for your physio and the next challenge to give you.
A transition to the front seat of your car.
You did great, and our first outing shouldn't be too far.
Go, baby, you have got this, and I am so impressed.
Each day I see you progress I am a little less stressed.

4.11.19

Twelve weeks tonight, babe, and day 84.
Still a while to go 'til you walk through the door.
Today you are depressed and struggling quite a bit
Your words to me were, "I feel like shit."
Your time away from home is playing in your head.
You feel like lying there, and not getting out of bed.
We all have crappy days and don't feel our best.
But each day you get up you pass another test.
You have got this, babe, I have faith and trust.
You coming home is an absolute must.

4.12.19

Day 85, another week has gone.
I'm still counting the days 'til we get you back home.
The last three months have flown by so fast.
I'm learning life is short and to treat
each day as if it is your last.
So the guitar I grabbed with my book of songs
and headed to room 11 so we could all sing along.
Kevin has family who are all very friendly.
We all sat around and listened to a music medley.
Our country songs and band camp atmosphere
had other patients pull up in wheelchairs so they could all hear.
It put a smile on the faces, especially you and me.
The best medicine outside laughter is music therapy.

4.13.19

Hey, baby, day 86, you're heading towards a tonne.
Every day I get up, you have me on the run.
It's Saturday, and most people are enjoying a weekend.
I'm running so much, I'm not sure what
is around the next bend.
I get calls all through the night.
You are very unsettled and often wake with a fright.
As a last resort, the nurses call my mobile.
It's dark and late, and the nurses' efforts
to settle you are all futile.
It takes me a while to calm you and get you back to bed.
Then at least another hour to switch off the
thoughts that are in my own head.
I do my best each day to walk in with a smile.
No matter how hard the night was, you look
at me and make it all worthwhile.

4.14.19

Day 87, and a huge day for you.
We finally get to take you out of RU!
Your progress to date has earned you a pass,
so the kids and I get to take you out to the park.
A picnic was made with sandwiches and treats.
You were so excited; it really was so sweet.
You got to sit in your beloved Colorado.
You didn't really care where you got to go.
You watched the boats as they sailed on by.
The joy on your face bought a tear to my eye.
Such a simple pleasure we all took for granted.
Today was the start of new memories to be planted.
It was short and sweet, only two hours long.
We ate, we laughed, and we listened to country songs.
It was a huge step forward to getting you back home.
It won't be long, Bub, 'til you are home where you belong.

4.15.19

Hey, Bub, another week started and day 88.
For your discharge date I cannot wait.
Off to the Gold Coast again today,
to see Dr Alt and her energetic ways.
Today's task was to start the brain remapping.
Silently inside, I could not stop clapping.
Your emotions and memory are currently conflicted,
meaning for you, holding thoughts is very much restricted.
This was a big one and started with two separate patterns.
Now ten days we wait to see what starts to happen.
I trust the universe and all Doctor Alt does.
And know, babe, all this I do with love.
So rest and recover, and try to relax.
And as from day 1, I still have your back.

4.16.19

Hey, baby, day 89, and each day you get stronger.
I'm counting the days; it won't be too much longer.
Some days are hard and a bit of a struggle.
I'd love nothing more than to lie in bed and just cuddle.
I know you are frustrated, and today I can really tell.
But I can't let you see me cry, even when at me you yell.
I've done my best to ensure your dignity.
And I promise, babe, I try to act with integrity.
Today you got mad at occupational therapy.
And when she left the room, you took it out on me.
I know it's hard when you feel treated like a child.
No matter how hard I tried to explain, you still got very wild.
Your independence, for now, is not quite your own.
And for your own safety, you cannot be left alone.
You know you can shower and go to the toilet.
But doing so unassisted is not safe for you just yet.
The time will come, Bub, when you will be nice and strong.
But you have to trust us and just play along.
I admire your courage, strength, and fight.
But tonight I'm going to bed and trying not to cry.

4.17.19

Hey, Bub, three months today, and it's gone so fast.
At the beginning, I wondered how we would last.
But each day I see you getting stronger,
and with physio, each day the walks are getting longer.
Your memory is still a worry,
but in all other strengths, you are getting better in a hurry.
Your speech and occupational therapist
work with you daily and put you to the test.
It's sad to see to the look in your eye
when you don't recall who dropped by.
The memory is not retaining.
It seems your brain will need retraining.
It's all about time and priorities.
I have no doubt it will all fall into place, eventually.
You have gotten this far, Bub, and I know there's more to go.
But no matter what, the kids and I love you, very much so.

4.18.19

Hey, Bub, thirteen weeks tonight
since you went down and gave us all a fright.
Today I spent the best seventy bucks yet.
I walked to Target and bought you a small television set.
Your eyes lit up; you were so delighted.
And it made my day to see you so excited.
Such a simple pleasure that we take for granted.
You thought all your wishes had just been handed.
Your sweet innocence and new emotional state
have me thanking the stars; you are my soul mate.
Thank you, baby, for being who you are.
I love you lots and need you to know you are my shining star!

4.19.19

Good Friday, and boy what a day.
Another step closer to having you home to stay.
Early this morning I stole you away,
and the kids and I took you home for Easter Good Friday.
It was very emotional and such a treat.
Our dogs Nugget and Molly were so excited they almost peed.
Nugget couldn't contain his excitement,
and he yelled and he screamed.
And Molly was so nice to you, I thought it was a dream.
We had a great day but very tiring for you.
By 3 p.m. you were exhausted, and we headed back to the RU.
Baby steps are all we need and progress moving forward.
I know it won't be long, and you will be home with us for good.

4.20.19

Day 93, and boy did we pay for yesterday's home stay.
You didn't sleep a wink last night; I'm not sure what to say.
I was awake all night and had several phone calls.
The nurses did their best to settle you and stop any falls.
Your brain got overstimulated, and it wouldn't slow down.
You kept the nurses busy and woke other patients all around.
I lost count at nine phone calls that
you don't remember making.
I felt so sad for you; I heard it in your voice
and how much you were shaking.
When I finally arrived at RU with my Easter bunny ears,
I had my basket laden with chocolate,
and it bought you to tears.
It made my day as you proudly handed Easter eggs out.
The smile it brought to other patients'
faces made it worth the shout.

4.21.19

Hey, baby, a big day ahead.
You will get to have a rest in your own bed.
Another home visit for Easter Sunday.
A little step closer to coming home to stay.
Lots of visitors and fun at home,
but we still need to be with you; you cannot be left alone.
Homemade scones and a roast × 2
Gave you a full belly before going back to RU.
You were showered, shaved, and put into bed.
And I braced myself like mad for the night that lay ahead.
Gotta say, Bub, you pleasantly surprised me.
Maybe it was the lavender and chamomile tea.
You slept like a log with no phone calls home.
It won't be long, baby, 'til you are not alone.

4.22.19

Hey, baby, we are heading to a hundred days fast.
No one knew how long this would last.
I have to say, "Take as long as you need."
And going forward, every sign we will heed.
I am impressed you slept really well last night.
No phone calls home or waking with a fright.
So tonight we will do the same with a hot cup of tea.
I hope this ensures a good sleep for both you and me.
Rest up, baby, the days are so long.
It won't be long 'til you are home where you belong.

4.23.19

Hey, Bub, a lazy day for you
as Tuesdays are conference calls at RU.
Your team of therapists is quite impressed,
both at your determination and at your rapid progress.
They are starting to look at assessing our home.
It won't be too long now, and we won't be sleeping alone.
For thirteen weeks you slept alone in your bed,
and the late-night dreams you had come to dread.
It's getting easier; you are settling on the phone.
I think it is comforting to hear my voice at home.
Each day it's getting easier, and you are sleeping more.
It won't be long now until you walk through our door.

4.24.19

Hey, baby, day 97, and only one phone call to me.
I still wake worrying, and I don't settle easily.
You are now off the extra day nurse and going it alone.
Another step closer to you coming home.
But at 2 p.m., when I visit, you are still in your PJs.
Seems communication and understanding went a little astray.
I felt so bad for you, and you kept saying, "Sorry."
Bub, it's not your fault; please do not worry.
I gave the nurses a chat, and we are of the same mindset.
We will get you into a routine, just a little time yet.
It's your memory and lack of understanding;
it will take a little more time and a little bit of diary planning.
I'll have the nurses remind you of your daily task.
I know over time they won't have to ask.
I love you lots, and you are really doing great.
Just know for you to come home, we all cannot wait.

4.25.19

Today we remember ANZACS and all that they have done.
But no dawn service for you; a home visit for some fun.
It's been a good day with a few visitors to see,
mixed with a little quiet time for you, the kids, and me.
Megan and Luke saw you walk and got a big cuddle too.
Because without them, there would be no longer you.
Every day is closer to you coming home.
It won't be long, babe, and you won't be sleeping alone.
I love you lots, and every day is a gift.
Life will be so different after this huge universal shift.

4.26.19

Hey, baby, one more day until you crack the tonne.
I am so proud of you; look how far you have come.
You have had a social day with a lot of laughs
and a special visit with a blast from the past.
An old school friend dropped in to see you.
You've still got some memory; you knew it was Andrew.
We laughed a while, and you reminisced.
Even though it's been years, it was like nothing was missed.
It was lovely to see but sad you didn't recall.
Cos five minutes after he left, you don't
remember him being there at all.
I know this is your challenge, and you don't know,
but every single visitor you have I take a photo.
I'll put it all together and combine it in a book
They will be there for you forever; all you have to do is look.

4.27.19

Hey, Bub, still going and a hundred days strong.
I am so impressed each day at how far you have come.
The memory is still an issue, or the lack thereof.
So today I implemented a dairy to help as a memory log.
After nine calls to me in just an hour,
I am really hoping this diary helps give back your power.
I'll get the nurses to take you to your board,
and each day note what therapy you have going on in the ward.
From physio to speech and occupational therapy,
I am hoping this diary will help towards
you retaining memory.
It will take patience and a little more time,
but babe, you have got this; it won't be long,
and you will be home and mine.

4.28.19

Hey, Bub, another family outing for a Sunday.
We dropped into Redcliffe for breakie on the way.
Our first family breakfast with Uncle Petie and Aunty Lee Lee,
Chantelle and Liam also joined, along with you and me.
We laughed, we ate, and we enjoyed the company,
then sat out on the veranda and looked out at the sea.
We don't realise what we actually have access to
until you have a change, such as what has happened to you.
We take so much for granted then realise who has your back.
I have to say I am grateful to Uncle Petie and
Aunty Lee Lee for keeping me on track.
They have been my emotional and spiritual
support, unconditionally.
Without them, I can honestly say I
don't know where I would be.
The universe brings us the right people if we accept.
I know going forward these two angels in my life will be kept.

4.29.19

What a big day you have had at day 102.
Your niece flew in from Canberra to visit you at RU.
Kirsty hadn't seen you outside of intensive care.
She was pleasantly surprised at first, and all she did was stare.
The last she had heard was the doctors said it was dire.
Now she stands in front of you with absolute admire.
I chatted with her for hours, telling of your journey
and how hard you have fought to come
back to the kids and me.
Every day you are getting stronger.
Keep going, Bub; it won't be too much longer.

4.30.19

Hey, Bub, day 103, and a jam session in your room.
It was very musical, with *boom, boom, boom*.
The room was full with Kirsty, Rhonda, and Billy.
While Kevin and I all played guitar, and we all sang happily.
It was a beautiful way to pass the day,
And music is a fantastic therapy.
You have to make the best of any situation.
To those who help you through it, show your appreciation.
So thank you, Kevin, for making it a pleasure.
The friendship we found in you, Conrad
and I will always treasure.

5.1.19

Hey, baby, we are now into May.
I feel this month you will be home to play.
Your physio and occupational therapists
did a home assessment today
to check out what needs to happen to get you home to stay.
I think they were impressed at everything we have done,
and even more so at how far you have come.
With very few recommendations and a few handrails,
I'm working the list and the minor details.
The best news though is it won't delay your discharge date.
I tell you, baby, we are all exited, and we cannot wait.
You are on the downhill run; I'm guessing under four weeks.
It's not long now, Bub, until you are home for keeps.

5.2.19

Fifteen weeks. Wow, time is rolling by.
I often turn up now, and you immediately start to cry.
You have been on a long journey, and at times one very scary.
The road has been so bumpy and very hairy.
We have all had lots of emotions running through our head,
but to see you so upset breaks my heart as you cry in your bed.
I don't know where you will recover to, and I don't really care.
As far as I am concerned, you are already there.
I am so proud of you and the progress so far.
In the kids' and my eyes, you are a shining star.

5.3.19

It's a happy and sad day here at RU.
Kevin has gone home and left me and you.
He has been a great support and a fantastic friend.
He has also been awesome at helping you mend.
With guitar in hand and a song in his head,
we often played at night while you lay in your bed.
I'm very happy he's going home,
but also sad as you feel so alone.
It won't be long, Bub, you will be doing the same.
Just like Kevin did, you gotta play the game.
Tomorrow you get to go home for three whole days.
This will be a test for us both to see your new ways.
Rest up, baby, I will pick you up at eight.
I am so excited and look forward to our breakie date.

(332)

5.4.19

Hey, baby, we're getting closer to having you back home.
Guess what, Bub, tonight we are not sleeping alone.
Your first weekend pass means a sleep in your bed.
Tonight there will be no phone calls I need to dread.
You have said for weeks, "Get me home,
I will sleep; that's all I need."
I tell you now, this threat I say, you better heed.
You had better sleep, or I will kick your ass.
Otherwise, I will take you back to RU real fast!
These are all steps to getting you home.
It won't be long, Bub, no more sleeping alone.

5.5.19

Day 108, and your first full night at home,
and the first in months of not sleeping alone.
You tossed and turned and was awake most of the night.
You were hot then cold and woke with a fright.
You were thirsty and wrestled and needed a piss.
This was worse than the phone calls I thought I wouldn't miss.
I felt so bad for you; you were so very tired.
But being at home had you out of sorts
and you brain over wired.
It's going to take time to get back to routine.
The sleepless nights I will handle to have
you back with the kids and me.

6.6.19

Hey, Bub, the end of our first weekend pass.
You did really well; there was nothing more I could ask.
I think we have got this; we will do just fine.
To find our new normal will just take time.
I'm not saying this will be easy; it's a learning curve.
I will do all I can to give you what you deserve.
I've handed in my notice at work to become your support.
It's the best, I feel, and needed; it's what I thought.
I'll be right beside you as you walk down this road.
And anytime you struggle, I will do
my best to lighten the load.
You are my husband, my love, and my life.
I'll do all I can, Bub, to be your carer but also your wife.

5.7.19

Hey, honey, today's the day we've been waiting for—
an adjusted date to walk out RU's door.
June 18 they said when you first arrived.
That's almost nine weeks ago, and we have survived.
So today as we sat waiting, it was a guessing game.
But our faces lit up when the doctors came.
I was hopeful of a new date towards the end of May
to get you back home for a permanent stay.
We both burst into tears at what the doctor advised.
OMG, babe, four weeks earlier is your date revised.
I knew you were progressing at a fantastic rate,
but this is awesome, now the twenty-first of May.
Fourteen days, Bub, that's only two weeks away.
I'm so proud of you; not long now and you'll be home to stay.

5.8.19

Hey, Bub, what a long, draining day.
I've worked and worked and then headed your way.
It's finally starting to sink in that you'll be home soon,
to find our new normal and sleep in your own room.
I spent three hours today just filling out your application.
Part of NDIS paperwork to continue your rehabilitation.
It was confronting in parts noting your abilities,
but it's needed to ensure support for your future disabilities.
I know it will get easier over time.
But it scared me, Bub, will you ever get back to being mine?
I know in your heart you love me; I know you do.
I worry, babe, will it again be me and you?
Thirty-one years together, twenty-five as husband and wife.
I'm just not sure what the future holds for our new life.
I love you with all my heart, and I know we will be okay.
We'll just walk this path together and take it day by day.

5.9.19

Hey, baby, day 112 with 12 to go.
The kids and I are so excited, we need you to know.
Our journey has been long and tiresome.
But just look at you and how far you have come.
I struggle to wipe the smile off my face.
I am so proud of you; you are winning this race.
Home tomorrow for another weekend pass.
I tell you now, if you don't sleep, I will kick your ass.
The last few nights I've had no calls.
You are finally learning to sleep within RU walls.
So another good night's sleep will do you great.
I'll pick you up tomorrow; I can't wait.

5.10.19

Hey, baby, we're mulling down the days fast.
Before we know it, day 124 will also be in the past.
Another weekend I get to take you home.
It won't be long, Bub 'til you are not sleeping alone.
Eleven days to go, and you'll be home for good.
Not everyone believed in you, and Bub, maybe they should.
Never underestimate the value of hope and love.
And always trust in the angels and higher powers from above.
I never doubted you and what you were capable of.
And I thank you with all my heart, which is so full of love.
Our journey has taught the kids and me
to never go down without a fight,
and to trust your inner guidance to lead you to what is right.

5.11.19

Hey, baby, a beautiful Saturday you got to spend at home.
Last night you slept in your bed, you weren't alone.
It will take a little getting used to, getting back on track.
To find your new normal; but babe, we've got your back.
You've found a routine and structure at RU.
I'll do all I can to make it easier for you.
We're working through the house to make it easier all around
and do our best to ensure you don't fall to the ground.
We will be with you 24/7 to ensure you are safe.
It's only ten days now 'til you are back in your place.

5.12.19

Hey, baby, day 115, and Happy Mother's Day to me.
We took you to Redcliffe for a family breakie.
It was our first family outing, and it was a lovely day.
Only nine more days until you are home to stay.
You've done amazing so far, but still a way to go.
The kids and I are so proud of you,
and we wanted you to know.
We are counting down the days on a calendar on the wall.
Not long now, Bub, not long at all.

5.13.19

Hey, baby, are you sick of my poems?
They are getting a little boring; you need to come home.
Every day I've tried to journal your story
cos you are not retaining thoughts or your short-term memory.
So each day I write it in a poem
and send updates to friends until you are home.
I'm running out of words, and to me, I'm getting boring.
Maybe I should stop writing and do you a drawing.
Umm, maybe not as I can't drawer for shit.
I think if I did, you'd die of a laughing fit.

5.14.19

Hey, baby, one week out; that's seven more sleeps
'til you are home with the kids and me for keeps.
Todays' poem I'll try to keep short and sweet
cos I feel each day I am on repeat.
As I have always said, I am so proud of you.
Not long now 'til you leave RU.
I am going to miss the drive,
and I know each day you will continue to thrive.
The doctors are super-impressed.
But our next challenge is for you to remember to get dressed.
The kids and I are grateful as you gain
physical strength each day.
And this is the reason you're finally coming home to stay.

5.15.19

Hey, Bub, today you have been moved.
You are not happy and nearly hit the roof.
You can't understand, and you are very unsure
why they have moved you to a room with beds for four.
We've done well to date in a single room
from the first hospital and all through RU.
You have also had one-on-one nurses to ensure you are safe.
And I can't complain, that's 118 days.
I feel the doctors are also testing you
and testing you with a change
to see how you manage when things we rearrange.
You really got unsettled and lost your crap.
According to you, you feel they gave you a bad rap.
Suck it up, princess, it's not long now.
You should be proud of yourself, so take a bow.

5.16.19

Hey, Bub, 119 days, and we are nearly there.
I've really started to think about this book I need to share.
Your journey has been interesting, and
I wouldn't want to do it again.
But I am looking forward to the future that is about to begin.
We've been happy, we've been grateful, and we've been sad.
The last four months have been the
biggest learning I have ever had.
The new direction for me is something
I've always wanted to approach,
that's to work and grow myself as an alternate life coach.
I listen and I care, and I want to help people change.
I also understand to others, I seem a little strange.
Guess what, Bub, I really don't care.
This is the beginning, and I will get there!

5.17.19

Day 120, and I am excited about what is around the corner.
It will be so good to have you home
with our sons and daughter.
We won't miss the daily drive and the
hours sitting at your bedside.
I have never doubted you in this roller-coaster ride.
I am overwhelmed with gratitude
and impressed at your never say die attitude.
The kids and I are so proud of you,
with only a few more sleeps at RU.

5.18.19

Day 121, and the last of your weekend passes.
Now my job will be to set up home therapy classes.
This next challenge for me will be to find the right therapist,
someone who will push you hard to bring out your best.
I know you will embrace the new routine ahead.
All I hope for is a good night's sleep in your own bed.
It's been great having you home
and both of us not sleeping alone.
But the sleepless nights for both will wear us down.
We have to find a routine and turn this around.
I hope you rest tonight, your third last at the PA.
It's only three more sleeps until you are back home to stay.

5.19.19

It's getting close now to the next chapter in our story.
I have to say thank you for all that you have taught me.
You helped me find my balance and see from a different side.
You challenged me daily on this not so fun ride.
I am very excited at what I have learnt so far.
And to me, you are the biggest and brightest shining star.
I am also very grateful for our family who have passed over,
especially my dad and your beautiful grandmother.
I appreciate their guidance and helping me stay sound.
And in the early days, they were the only support I found.
Without them I am not sure if I could have stayed so strong.
According to doctors and some others, I had this all so wrong.
As I write this poem, I smile at how you proved them wrong
as after just four months and four days, you
will be home where you belong.

5.20.19

Hey, Bub, one more sleep 'til you leave the RU.
It seems like only yesterday you were in the ICU.
The doctors back then had given up hope.
But you know me, I was adamant; it was nope.
I'm so grateful to the universe above
And for you fighting so hard for our love.
I never had a doubt; I knew you were there.
Now I understand this journey I needed to share.
So each day that I've written you a poem
Will be a big part of my new journey
when you come back home.
My guides and angels have again made me look.
Apparently this now needs to be written in a book.
I started to resist and say, "No, I'm not a writer."
But according to them, I need to listen,
and stop being a fighter.
So I'm committed, I'm learning, and it's a great feeling.
The book is going to be called *124 Days of Hope and Healing*!

5.21.19

Hey, baby, 124 days of hope and healing.
I can't explain this overwhelming feeling.
Our journey so far has been a long one,
but I also know there is another one to come.
The hospital visits and overnight stays
will now become therapies at home each weekday.
We'll find our new normal and steady routines.
And that's okay, Bub, at least you are
home with the kids and me.
We love you so much, and we are so proud of you
cos today is the day that you leave the RU!

Printed in the United States
By Bookmasters